B
LEVY

McK
195

Blue

D0571781

5/06

$22.00

DATE			

WALTHAM
PUBLIC LIBRARY

BAKER & TAYLOR

WALTHAM
PUBLIC LIBRARY

Blue Peninsula

Blue Peninsula

ESSENTIAL WORDS FOR A
LIFE OF LOSS AND CHANGE

Madge McKeithen

FARRAR, STRAUS AND GIROUX

NEW YORK

Farrar, Straus and Giroux
19 Union Square West, New York 10003

Copyright © 2006 by Madge McKeithen
All rights reserved
Distributed in Canada by Douglas & McIntyre Ltd.
Printed in the United States of America
First edition, 2006

Owing to limitations of space, all acknowledgments for permission
to reprint previously published material appear on pages 213–219.

Library of Congress Cataloging-in-Publication Data
McKeithen, Madge, 1955–
    Blue peninsula : essential words for a life of loss and change /
Madge McKeithen.— 1st ed.
        p.   cm.
    ISBN-13: 978-0-374-11502-9 (hardcover : alk. paper)
    ISBN-10: 0-374-11502-8 (hardcover : alk. paper)
    1. Levy, Isaac—Health. 2. McKeithen, Madge, 1955–
3. Brain—Degeneration—Patients—Biography. 4. Parents of
children with disabilities—Biography. 5. Mothers and sons—
Biography.   I. Title.

RC394.D35M35 2006
362.196′80092—dc22

                                                2005024281

Designed by Cassandra J. Pappas

www.fsgbooks.com

1   3   5   7   9   10   8   6   4   2

for Ike and Nick and Noah

and

for Abigail Thomas

At length, in a nook of the river, gloomy with the weight of overhanging foliage, and still and deep as a soul in which the torrent eddies of pain have hollowed a great gulf, and then subsiding in violence, have left it full of a motionless fathomless sorrow— I saw a little boat lying.

—GEORGE MacDONALD

Contents

Preface

La poésie ne s'impose plus, elle s'expose.
—PAUL CELAN

In writing this book, the preface marks the end. It is the last piece to write in this book I would wish not to write, just as I would wish, more than any desire I have known, my son not to be sick. Now that the other pieces are written, it is harder to leave the writing than it was to begin, hard to wrap it up and let it go, for in it I have found companionship. My son's illness goes on, and my life with it does, and no reaching for things that help will change that reality. But then, I knew that. This book is not about resolution, but about connection. What I have to offer you is my passionate belief in these poems—works that have been powerful in a despair that I would not wish on anyone yet know is not uniquely mine.

Why poems? Scholars and poets can answer that question more profoundly than I. From experience, I say simply that they speak in a way I can hear, be it their accessibility, music, figurative language, their offer of a suggestion rather than a proof, works of art not argument, moving subtly yet powerfully and often in spite of me. Poems insinuate themselves. They get through when other things cannot.

Why *my* take in this way on these poems? Perhaps this book will ring true for you because of my passion and my pain rendered as I have been able, and you will find here something you need, maybe a surprise. Early on in the writing, a fellow poetry lover said, "I see what you're doing—with poetry you are trying to make sense of your chaos." Who isn't?

I wanted to create something that could be put into the hands of someone facing the unknown, the way I was with Ike eight years ago now, in the fall of 1997, and so many times since. The divide between health and illness feels vast. Without a diagnosis, without understanding of cause or origin, the bridge is out. Suspension continues without visible supports. At first I thought I would simply compile the poems and that their usefulness would be self-evident. "Here! See?" But if poems handed to friends had needed context, how could I expect it to be different with people I had never met? Friends have wanted to know why this poem from this person at this time, and then they get it the way *they* get it, which is the point. Not my way, but my way as a place from which to agree or to diverge—the beginning of a dialogue.

So, this book is my part of a dialogue in which I hope you will engage. Perhaps a poem will reach you, or an approach to a poem, a way of listening to one or thinking about another, a meeting of the minds, or an engagement in disagreement. Poetry can be read and reread and yield fresh, unexpected things, even for the same reader at repeat readings.

Poetry and grief demand their pace. They ask me to be still and listen while they deliver and develop, but not for too long. My experiences and what came to me in them are offered to deliver you to the thresholds of poems that will take you on from there. In the writing of these essays, I had the recurring image of putting all the leaves back on a tree that was bare in midwinter, so that once they were all in place, the wind could do its thing, as if once done, the undoing would be better allowed.

The first piece, "A Coming to Terms," tells the bulk of my son Ike's eight-year experience with degenerative neurological disorders of unknown genesis. Beyond the first piece, the book can be read in any order. The pieces and the poetry make a whole, but it can be dipped into and put down and then picked up again later. I hope this book will go with you to waiting rooms, exam rooms, daily places, and places that interrupt and dislodge the routine. Reading it in pieces brings limits to mind—how I can do only so much in so much time before needing to look up to see the river that is carrying me and to remember the world beyond.

I have tried not to belabor and not to give in to the facile. Although my upbringing was Christian, my religious and spiritual beliefs are cobbled together. I am no saint, I have misbehaved more than a little, and I have not been noble in the face of what has come my way. Some who have suffered nobly have crossed my path, and a few of their stories are in these pages. I am a scrapper who believes that we are meant to live before we die, and if we are fortunate, while we die. What that living means reshapes itself along the way. My life was one thing and is now another, or rather many others, in part because of the appearance and unrelenting persistence of a son's illness. I suspect the same blown-apart multiplicity is true for you, though coming with your own particular explosion.

An inspiring off-Broadway play was recently promoted by the producer, who claimed that she was telling all the "important people" in town to go see it. Her choice of words was ironic, for the heart of the play was about "unimportant people," the marginalized and disenfranchised. Yet her words were right on target, the play and her promotion of it bringing the marginalized front and center before the brokers of the cultural mainstream.

Illness and disability marginalize people. This may become less so as the aging of our huge baby boom generation redefines "normal." Even so, the world continues to be predicated largely on assumptions of health. If the illness or condition is rare or not well understood, those affected can feel like third cousins twice-removed, so distant no one can be bothered. Poems can return the ill to the fold. These poems were not retrieved from grieving manuals or collections of poetry for the infirm. They were found piecemeal and in what I usually read and what that reading led to. Some of them are familiar, found in major anthologies and journals; others are less well-known. Hearing them speak to me and for me pulled me back from the exiled margins, the poet reaching where little else could.

At a point in writing this book, I contacted one of the poets, asking if he would tell me after I had written a piece if I had "gotten it right." He replied that once created, his works stand on their own, fend for themselves; he thanked me for believing in his work and wished me well. His reply was generous—the poet getting out of the way of his creation, refusing to obsess, control, or hyper-manage. How wonderful it would be to be his child, guided and let go, affirmed and believed in.

No attempt has been made to say that these are the absolute best poems to read in an experience of grief or sorrow. Another writer early on in my process of creating this work mentioned that with just the poems, without the pieces of memoir, it would be a bit of a quirky collection. My hunch is that now, with the pieces of Ike's story, it still has aspects of quirkiness. In a way, that is fitting. In its most common definition, a *quirk* is a sudden turn or twist, a deviation from the regular course. The illness has had plenty of quirks. Poems have an uncanny power to turn me, to shift the reader, what Robert Frost called their *twinkle*. In carpentry and plastering, there are also *quirks*—small channels, deeply recessed in proportion to their width, used to insulate and give relief to convex rounded moldings. The poems have certainly provided space and insulation and relief against the stresses of illness. So, quirky charged? Quirky claimed.

At the least, in my portion of the dialogue that is this book, I hope that I have done no harm—to the rich experience of poetry or to those of you who may look for yourselves in these pages. At best, I hope that this book will go with you into the margins and maybe at times provide a bridge of words and experiences. I trust that these poems, and how they find you and how you *get* them, leave you neither lonelier nor more lost, and that they engage you, even absent answers. The poems may leave you wanting, which, when you consider it, is vastly better than not.

Blue Peninsula

A Coming to Terms

A MATHEMATICS OF BREATHING

I

Think of any of several arched
colonnades to a cathedral,

how the arches
like fountains, say,

or certain limits in calculus,
when put to the graph-paper's cross-trees,

never quite meet any promised heaven,
instead at their vaulted heights

falling down to the abruptly ending
base of the next column,

smaller, the one smaller
past that, at last

dying, what is
called perspective.

This is the way buildings do it.

II

You have seen them, surely, busy paring
the world down to what it is mostly,

proverb: so many birds in a bush.
Suddenly they take off, and at first

it seems your particular hedge itself
has sighed deeply,

that the birds are what come,
though of course it is just the birds

leaving one space for others.
After they've gone, put your ear to the bush,

listen. There are three sides: the leaves'
releasing of something, your ear where it

finds it, and the air in between, to say
equals. *There is maybe a fourth side,*

not breathing.

III

In my version of the Thousand and One Nights,
there are only a thousand,

Scheherazade herself is the last one,
for the moment held back,

for a moment all the odds hang even.
The stories she tells she tells mostly

to win another night of watching the prince
drift into a deep sleeping beside her,

the chance to touch one more time
his limbs, going,

gone soft already with dreaming.
When she tells her own story,

Breathe in,
breathe out

is how it starts.

—Carl Phillips

My son's illness is eight years old and has no name. It started when he was fourteen. He is now twenty-two. It is taking away his ability to walk and to reason. It is getting worse, some years more rapidly than others. Doctors continue to look for a name to call it. Until they find one, it is known to us by the names of its symptoms—progressive spastic paraparesis, Bence-Jones proteinuria, subcortical dementia—and intimately by its subtle violence, the anonymous thief ravaging our dreams and twisting our son's life.

falling down to the abruptly ending
base of the next column,

smaller, the one smaller
past that . . .

He had been healthy and characteristically happy, our firstborn. Isaac, we had named him, "the one who laughs"; he chose to be called Ike when he became a teenager. During the second half of 1997, as he approached his fifteenth birthday, his walk became stiff-legged, progressively awkward, lurching. The pediatrician referred us to an orthopedist and he to a neurologist. November 13, 1997, a Thursday afternoon, the brilliant pediatric neurologist who would pursue the first battery of tests examined Ike and said, almost to himself, "There is definitely something wrong here." We had begun the leap across the divide from "before" and "normal." We had no idea that eight years later we would still be suspended, waiting for an "after," a diagnosis, a place to land.

The first symptoms were progressive spastic paraparesis. Paraparesis is *paresis*, incomplete paralysis, and *para*, of the lower body. *Spastic*, his legs are stiff, brick-hard, and they do not move well at the knee, the ankle, or the hip. More recently, they often become entangled. He twists himself up, falls. Hyperreflexia, abnormal Babinski: Ike's toes fan up and out when the sole of his foot is stroked by the doctor's hammer, the classic indicator of a major problem in the central nervous system's corticospinal tract. Ike's legs have too much tone and excessive reflexes; his inhibitory impulses are impaired. More now, there are repetitive tremors and bounces that last for several minutes. Sometimes he tells me that these more sustained tremors are beginning to hurt. *Progressive*, it is getting worse. He has gone from walking with only an apparent limp, to a lurching, lunging walk using walls and railings, to the use of a cane or walker and scooter or wheelchair. He can walk only a single city block now. His pulse races with the effort. It is hard to avoid imagining a time when he will be unable to walk, period.

More than forty disorders on the original differential diagnosis were considered and eliminated in the first months. Brain and spine MRIs, a skin-muscle biopsy, blood tests, gene scans—I sensed that we were in good hands. I was completely unprepared for no answer, for uncertainty, silence. I simply did not know that "none of the above" was among the multiple choices of modern medicine. Naïve, perhaps, but I am not alone in this. When friends asked about a diagnosis and we replied, "Nothing clear yet," their looks showed disbelief. Surely we had not been to the right doctors, asked the right questions, used the right words.

Obvious things were quickly ruled out. No lesions. No family history of degenerative disorders. Tests continued. Fibroblasts from the skin-muscle biopsy were stored here, tested there. Little pieces of our son flew everywhere. "Orphan diseases," rare and rarely well funded, entered my vocabulary. My Web browser "favorites" list grew long with rare disorder Web sites. We followed up on each hint of a treatable condition, as well as the untreatable, valuing even a name for the unidentified intruder. We flew to New York and Philadelphia and the Mayo Clinic and discussed Ike's case on the phone with specialists in Durham, Baltimore,

D.C., New York, Ann Arbor, and Boston. I took Ike to physical and psychological therapists—and to back specialists. He and I took up swimming after school to strengthen his back and maintain his mobility. I volunteered with an ALS patient and attended a national family conference for one of the orphan diseases for which Ike was being tested—to stare down my worst fears. I found heroes in places I had never wanted to go looking.

As we lived forward—at work and school, at home and in our community—slowly, almost imperceptibly, Ike worsened.

. . . so many birds in a bush.
Suddenly they take off . . .

Our coping depended on framing Ike's illness as static; to see it progressing was unbearable. Our relationship with our pediatric neurologist was understandably strained. A committed clinician, he reported what he saw, and what he saw was worsening. I knew he was too smart to be inaccurate. Ike said it was too depressing to go to see him, and so, for a while, we did not.

During Ike's senior year of high school, Bence-Jones proteinuria appeared in a routine exam. Substantial amounts of a kappa light-chain protein in his urine, and we were off and running again, new questions for the oracle. Hematology joined neurology among the medical specialties that might hold clues. More consults and scans and biopsies, a few more things ruled out, and a new "condition" named MGUS—monoclonal gammopathy of undetermined significance. Undetermined significance. More things "not normal," more indicators to monitor, yet no more understanding of cause or prognosis.

Ike left home for college in September 2001, four years into his illness, with a scooter to get around, a dormitory resident adviser who himself lived with a physical disability, and a learning support program, should he need it. No longer living with the day to day of Ike's illness, cut into by a friend's death in an automobile accident and by my small portion of the enormous grief of 9/11, in September, October, and November of 2001 my life reverberated with emptied-ness. I left full-time teaching and began to write, and as Pablo Neruda puts it,

> . . . *Poetry arrived*
> *in search of me.*

I became a poetry addict—collecting, consuming, ripping poems out of magazines, buying slender volumes that would fit in my pocket or pocketbook, stashing them in loose-leaf notebooks, on shelves, stacking them on the floor. In the midst of all this grief, I had fallen in love. With words. Poems, especially. And just in time.

On November 9, the college called. Ike was disoriented, confused, approaching paranoid. Enter the third symptom, dementia. Although most of his illness had been chronic, gradual, incremental, this was acute, a crisis. A detailed neuropsychological exam confirmed observations—marked cognitive decline in most areas, chunks of IQ lost, substantial drops in speed of processing, retrieval. Still no "*why*." College was gone, doctors' visits resumed; a new stage required our entrance. In June of 2003, six years into his illness, MRIs confirmed brain atrophy, loss of gray and white matter, and still no known cause.

. . . There is maybe a fourth side,
not breathing.

Poems became almost all I could read. I tucked them inside the thick file of Ike's medical records when we headed for Mayo again, then to a geneticist, and to Children's Hospital of Philadelphia. I read and reread them in waiting rooms and exam rooms and sometimes hid in them when the world I could touch was too much. Poems spoke to me and sometimes for me.

With a diagnosis, like it or not, you belong somewhere. Without a diagnosis, nowhere. There is no group for Those Waiting to Know. No national organization. No informational brochures. But you can curl up in a poem and sometimes find there what you need—a way to wait, humility, perspective, love—to go back out.

The poems I collected, at times near lifesaving in various stages of my son's illness, have again kept me company as I have been writing in recent months. I would not have considered writing about Ike's experience without these poems; with them, I can try to hold the gaze of examination and reflection. As I looked back through those I had collected over the years, I saw poems about creating a space, admitting vulnerability, the incompleteness of knowing, connecting through suffering, and finding energy and life in the midst of it all. Some have the feel of an unanswered question, some of a questioned answer. Some contain; some leak. Stopping short of or at a place other than with a complete answer can be abided when a poem goes with you. Poems can suggest and value incompleteness, the understanding that derives from partiality, the knowing in part that is both horrible and beautiful.

"Wait until another symptom develops, until something worsens," a doctor instructed. Asked to acknowledge such powerlessness relative to my son, I could not catch my breath. Now, sadly, eight years later, I know what the doctor meant. I could not have abided seeing it without the poet.

My son's symptoms are worse. The speed of the degeneration has picked up in the last year. Conversations with him do not now flow; they are more analogous to the work of mining gems or the haphazard discovery of shells at the water's edge, sometimes extracted with considerable effort, at other times stumbled upon. In this, "A Mathematics of Breathing" reminds me to keep breathing and shifting perspective and allowing for the possibility of new dreams.

Mathematics is about quantities and operations, amounts and processes. So is knowing—things known and ways of

knowing them. And so, this poem suggests, is breathing—
the fullness of life as well as its rhythms, in and out. Forms
abound in its lines—architecture, calculus limits, graph-
paper crosstrees, colonnades and vaults, equilateral triangles
and squares, a thousand nights and *the odds hang*[ing] *even*.
And processes—thinking, falling, dying, paring down, sigh-
ing, leaving, listening, releasing, finding, telling, watching,
sleeping, touching, dreaming.

Not breathing seems to me a sort of involuntary non-
movement, the holding of our breath that comes with intense fear or stress or sorrow. In the stillest, saddest places,
something from outside must coax movement. In words and
form, this poem does. *Breathe in, / breathe out . . .* these lines
draw attention. The lines are breathable pairs—inhales and
exhales—spread out, pulling air in. Not packed too densely,
the poem breathes and invites response.

It starts with the suggestion, *Think*, an offer to cross the
threshold and step inside. A colonnade stretches into the
distance. Eyes, tracing its lines and repetitions, move. There
are *certain limits* in a world of man-made structures, the territory we are used to. Arches and fountains fall down, and
the *promised heaven* is never quite met, but *vaulted heights*
are reached, and the colonnade does provide support; it
does hold up the cathedral. The *dying* in this poem is a perspective, a way things look given the parameters of space
and perception. In experiences of ongoing loss, in our son's
degenerative illness, this poem reimages the falling away.
Diminishing is dignified. Loss, illness, degeneration is placed

in an aesthetic order, validated by construction, *the way buildings do it.*

The second part of the poem moves closer with the more familiar *You have seen them, surely,* the poet standing next to the reader to look together at something familiar, to venture a new take on something already known. Honing, focusing in, *paring / the world down to what it is mostly,* the poem takes the reader to proverb, to "before a word," a known thing containing wisdom, sometimes puzzling but just the same an assumed truth. The "bird in hand worth two in the bush" proverb, and the birds taking off, as if the *particular hedge itself / has sighed deeply.* The poem constructs a triangle from the *releasing of something,* the awareness of that release and *the air in between*—Ike's reliable good health leaving, our admitting the sadness, and the time or space or whatever it is that is needed in between. Another equal side, the *fourth side, / not breathing.* From the loss to a perception of it, to traverse the . . . *air in between* . . . involves crossing a territory of *not breathing.*

Another way, the poem suggests. *In my version* . . . begins part III. Scheherazade is spinning out cliff-hangers for her very life. The reader has escaped the stock-still *not breathing* of the last line of part II for territory riddled with risk—odds, winning, chance—not just movement but creativity and inventiveness in the face of each day's dangers. Leaving denial to risk death daily, fending it off to stay alive for *the chance to touch one more time / his limbs, going, / gone soft already with dreaming*, and in that dreaming to envision the shore of a life shaped by illness.

The poem contains loss, risk, and continuing. It ends with the word *starts*, in a single inhale line. It offers life as a quantity to be held and asks the reader to breathe it in and out. The last line—*is how it starts*—draws the breath in. Ours is to exhale, respond, create . . . continue.

Acquiring Losses

ONE ART

The art of losing isn't hard to master;
so many things seem filled with the intent
to be lost that their loss is no disaster.

Lose something every day. Accept the fluster
of lost door keys, the hour badly spent.
The art of losing isn't hard to master.

Then practice losing farther, losing faster:
places, and names, and where it was you meant
to travel. None of these will bring disaster.

I lost my mother's watch. And look! My last, or
next-to-last, of three loved houses went.
The art of losing isn't hard to master.

I lost two cities, lovely ones. And, vaster,
some realms I owned, two rivers, a continent.
I miss them, but it wasn't a disaster.

—Even losing you (the joking voice, a gesture
I love) I shan't have lied. It's evident
the art of losing's not too hard to master
though it may look like (Write it!) like disaster.

—ELIZABETH BISHOP

*L**ose something every day.* Your world is a slowly contracting circle. You can picture that; it isn't hard to master. You can't keep track of things, so just give them up—your car, your cell phone, your computer. You can't explain yourself to people who knew you before, so just give them up—former friends. You can't run anymore; when you swim now, it's about your arms, your legs weighty, anchors—give it up. Sit. This losing must go farther, faster. This losing, finally something you can master, finally something I can master. All I have to give up is *where it was you meant / to travel*—just the dreams and hopes of what your life would be, my son, just its full, round shape, just the dream that you would stretch out into it as you grew and loved others and knew their love, the hope that you would sometimes share with me the sense you had made of things, of your world. But you won't be doing that, will you? . . . *disaster.*

Crying in the Car

POEMS MAY NOT GEYSER

Poems may not geyser
from the fount of the psyche
every time talking ends.
Chant begins in ribbed caverns
and builds to a simple faith
through a sacrament of song.

No, words may not always spurt
or well from their source,
even if they did until now,
and even though your voice
wraps anger in disappointment
in nonchalance in mission,
all wadded up in sound layers
delicate as mist, even though

your voice steps around
the fraying edges of a sigh.

Oh, I would flay the moment
for the scented bark of songs,
peel the ʒest from a mood,
even butcher the morning
for you, except that geysers
rarely spring from thirst,
but from earth, in gentle mayhem,
when deep humors churn
and words burst free.

—DIANE ACKERMAN

In Atlanta, a car-dependent city, I depended on my car as a place to cry. In the sliding-in-between time at the end of a workday, headed home to family in the years of Ike's illness, what often sprang up for me were tears. I could maintain at work and all the way to my car being cheerful for fellow teachers, calling out to students on the soccer field, returning their calls to me. I could maintain at church and social events, and when I was with anyone else in the car, I did not cry. But alone, everything pent up, everything *all wadded up in sound layers / delicate as mist . . .* all efforts to make things acceptable, that voice that *wraps anger in dis-*

appointment / in nonchalance in mission would give way to
the one that *steps around / the fraying edges of a sigh*. And the
gentle mayhem, / when deep humors churn would break into
weeping, sometimes with words, more often not.

In the quiet of the car, free of the obligation to speak to
anyone, free to listen to music or the radio or nothing at all,
tears would geyser. The dark humors of the medieval phys-
iologist were strained to clear tear waters. A wrung sponge,
I felt the strain.

Especially under the canopy of trees on West Wesley
Road, I would cry, between my school and my younger son
Nick's, after a day of teaching that had perhaps been inter-
rupted with phone calls from Ike because he had fallen or
with calls to doctors for test results or information. There
was this little window of time between the façade that had
been required of me at school and the façade that I needed
to have for Nick or for whatever was happening at Nick's
school; in that little window, I cried and sometimes sobbed.

The three cars I did that crying in are gone now—one
traded in hurriedly for safety reasons, one sold to a cousin
when Ike gave up driving, and the third sold when I moved
to New York and became for the first time in almost three
decades car free. Where will I cry now?

Last Thursday evening, close to dark, I saw a young
woman walking south on Columbus Avenue. I was headed
north. She was weeping, tears visibly streaking her cheeks,
and she was talking on her cell phone. I assumed a heart-

break, a breakup. In a pedestrian life in a city, maybe some crying is done in the open. On the subway the other day I wept when I read a letter with kind words about Ike's illness. A man and woman about my age came over to speak to me, to make sure I was okay. The tears surprised me, as did the people's response. A friend who has lived her entire life in New York City said it should not have, that people here care; they simply do not always look as if they would.

In my apartment alone, I weep looking at a picture of Ike on his U-Can-Go scooter going under Greywacke Arch in Central Park, riding not walking, east, not far from the hospital where he was born, twenty-two years ago. How quick has been the cycle from infancy to walking to not walking, a circle too tight, a vise. Today I wept in the Starbucks at Columbus and 76th over the lyrics to the song "The Weight"—words not inherently sad. Seated at the end of the counter near the wall, I turned my sadness toward the coffee-colored wallpaper, and I was angry at my tears. I wanted out. Give me indifference or a competing passion to outshine this one. Give me something other than this ongoing connection to pain in the past, present, and future tenses.

But where is what I started for, so long ago?
And why is it yet unfound?

—from "Facing West from California's Shores"
by WALT WHITMAN, *Leaves of Grass*, #27

Again a poem, and I can hold steady, continue for the not yet reached.

Perhaps not all holes are meant to be filled, nor weights to be lightened. Some have suggested that we were created with God-size holes in our hearts; Henri Nouwen, that no one is meant to be everything to us. Satiation is overrated. Things are yet unfound.

Clarity

MR COGITO AND THE IMAGINATION

I

Mr Cogito never trusted
tricks of the imagination

the piano at the top of the Alps
played false concerts for him

he didn't appreciate labyrinths
the Sphinx filled him with loathing

he lived in a house with no basement
without mirrors or dialectics

jungles of tangled images
were not his home

he would rarely soar
on the wings of a metaphor
and then he fell like Icarus
into the embrace of the Great Mother

he adored tautologies
explanations
idem per idem

that a bird is a bird
slavery means slavery
a knife is a knife
death remains death

he loved
the flat horizon
a straight line
the gravity of the earth

2

Mr Cogito will be numbered
among the species minores

he will accept indifferently the verdict
of future scholars of the letter

he used the imagination
for entirely different purposes

he wanted to make it
an instrument of compassion

he wanted to understand to the very end

- *Pascal's night*
- *the nature of a diamond*
- *the melancholy of the prophets*
- *Achilles' wrath*
- *the madness of those who kill*
- *the dreams of Mary Stuart*
- *Neanderthal fear*
- *the despair of the last Aztecs*
- *Nietzsche's long death throes*
- *the joy of the painter of Lascaux*
- *the rise and fall of an oak*
- *the rise and fall of Rome*

and so to bring the dead back to life
to preserve the covenant

Mr Cogito's imagination
has the motion of a pendulum

it crosses with precision
from suffering to suffering

there is no place in it
for the artificial fires of poetry

he would like to remain faithful
to uncertain clarity

—ZBIGNIEW HERBERT
(translated by John and Bogdana Carpenter)

One of the hardest things about Ike's illness—still—is making peace with the cognitive loss, how to grapple with staying connected when the connections that support thought and speech appear to be fraying. And when a peace is reached, it's momentary, tenuous. It has to be renegotiated and renegotiated again and again. Early in the stages of knowing that his degeneration was affecting his thinking, I sat alone in the small chapel at Covenant Presbyterian Church in Atlanta one Sunday morning before worship began in the main sanctuary and leafed through the prayers for special occasions at the back of the hymnal. Nothing helped in this particular agony of loving one who is losing his mind. So much of religious rhetoric seemed to rest on mind and word.

For a while I tried to be helped by the notion that the brain is an organ, an organ of the human body, like the liver or the pancreas or the bladder. But the trying did not work.

Mr. Cogito reduced the monster of my fear.

First, he showed me myself—adoring sense-making machinery while hearing that much sense making is non-sense—*tautologies / explanations / idem per idem*. And it was easier to go easy on Mr. Cogito, appealing, asking that things be what they are, simply wanting truth in advertising.

After a few readings, Mr. Cogito seemed to be Ike.

> *he loved*
> *the flat horizon*
> *a straight line*
> *the gravity of the earth*

Ike has always craved clarity. He likes clear-cut stories of good versus evil—where the good guys or at least the cool guys win—dramatic events in sports, blatant beauty, slapstick humor, and the color red. He is principally a concrete thinker. Briefly he crossed the threshold into more abstract conceptualizations and hypothetical reasoning, but the illness surfaced and he never proceeded far into that room. With his ability to hold on to straightforward logical sequences now perforated, the more adventurously imaginative seems a terrain he cannot occupy.

What Ike does now is to bring the imagined into his concrete. He blurs the line between suggested and actual. A pretty girl who smiles at him on the sidewalk is more than casually interested in him. Hand him a basketball, and in his head, he plays the game like LeBron James. Although he cannot tell the story that he just read—his sequencing now spotty—he imagines coauthoring a book with his favorite writer. A friend's passing comment, "You know you've been to a baseball game when you have the hat," becomes an imperative to Ike, and he will not leave the stadium without one. Ike's attraction to movies has a growing sense of hiding out, an understandable but troubling preference for the fictional world.

At casual encounter, it seems that Ike ought to be able to get over what seem silly, at times arrogant, affectations. Not understood, the particular faces of his degeneration can be maddening to others. It takes work to comprehend and to help others understand. Understanding diffuses the irritating aspects of his behavior a bit. Yet even when I know that I am seeing the unreasonable, the manifestations of his illness that make no sense, it is hard to dismiss his desires. The unreasonable unmet wishes of this one I love break my heart. Why *can't* he get what he wants? Find what he needs?

Mr. Cogito is not doing nothing. Not trusting tricks of the imagination, *he used the imagination / for entirely different purposes / he wanted to make it / an instrument of compassion / he wanted to understand to the very end* a host of circumstances—dark, brilliant, profound, fearful, desperate, joyous, and complex. From inside Ike's illness, he must have seen most of these things. From the outside, I have seen most of them in him. A friend recently said he had a real sense that Ike was there beyond his difficulties and lost abilities to communicate—there, a presence. That I cannot know he knows does not change his presence. Only my perception of it, something I can work on, to find what I need.

An instrument of compassion, yet terrible, is Ike's opening, what seems like letting go, allowing him to live more peacefully. Usually now, a mental struggle does not dominate. The actual and imagined wash back and forth, one over the other in his life. The letting go is not done yet, and its progress is erratic. He holds reality, as he understands it, to himself in his unique ways. He makes lists exhaustively—of movies he has seen, ones he wants to see, of CDs he has owned, of girls with whom he feels he has a connection, from girls he dated to movie stars he idolizes. Sometimes with a fringe of anxiety Ike off-loads his details to others—to me, his brother, his father, the people at Camphill Soltane, the community in eastern Pennsylvania where he lives ten months of the year. He sends me game tickets and programs and dates scribbled on papers to keep in his mementos file for him. But it is calmer now than earlier. Maybe, the poem suggests, it is easier to give it up if it was only, after all, *uncertain clarity*. To the extent that the world with this illness is becoming for Ike *jungles of tangled images / . . . not his home*, his degeneration is granting his childhood wish for things to be as they seemed, seamless from surface to core.

Like Mr. Cogito, Ike with this illness bucks the trend, follows his heart, and is fundamentally compassionate. At his most basic level Ike cares about others, not always in ways the world can see. Many of his actions fall outside the norms of expected courteous behavior. It is hard to believe that he likes people when he passes without speaking. He thinks he has spoken, but he does not realistically perceive himself in his environment. Anxious, I want to ask him to be thoughtful of others; then I listen to myself—*be* thought *full*, as if he could simply will it so. Frustrated, Ike's father, Noah, or I start the sentence—"Ike acts as if he's oblivious . . ."—and we stop short, realizing that Ike *is* in fact oblivious, without choice, to an increasing number of circumstances. Remembering and helping those around Ike to remember the "disconnect" between his behavior and his true feelings and intentions is important to his life going forward, to keeping him connected to others. That a behavior is thought-*less* is a tool for understanding him and not a judgment.

HOW YOU die out in me:

down to the last
worn-out
knot of breath
you're there, with a
splinter of
life.

—PAUL CELAN
(translated by MICHAEL HAMBURGER)

My hunch is that others see too that Ike is an insistent splinter of compassion beneath the tight, tired knots of his illness. When he rejoices, it is in small things—a new pair of shoes, a baseball cap. He loves in his own way, as we each do. I sense at times that he would like to love more openly, more flexibly. Others around him do, trying to reach him, trying to reach around the scattershot that his illness is throwing out. There are possibilities for Ike—at Soltane, at his church, at the senior living center where he volunteers, with family friends when he is with us. Sharp and defiant as the splinter in the poem, there is an Ike who remains and claims life when all else is burned away and dying out.

Oblivious and a-logical and compassionate, he continues in this world that he really would have imagined otherwise.

Looking

. . . loosen in me the hold of visible things
Help me to walk by faith and not by sight
. . . in the land of things that swell and seem,
Help me to walk by the other light supreme,
Which shows thy facts behind man's vaguely hinting
   dream.

—from "September 25," *Diary of an Old Soul,*
by GEORGE MACDONALD

I may be a terminal fence-sitter on the question of looking. People with opinions on the subject can be
grouped into two camps—those who believe that you see
most intensely and importantly with your eyes, and those
who claim that the most intense and important seeing is

beyond the eyes, a knowing or awareness not limited to corneal, retinal perceptions. In the course of Ike's illness, each type of looking and seeing has been key at different times.

Ike and Nick see in very different ways. Ike probably always needed glasses; each year at the pediatrician's he was hesitant in responding to questions during the eye exam. When he did get glasses, the afternoon before he started first grade, in the parking lot between the LensCrafters and the car he pointed up: "Look at the airplane!" He pointed straight ahead—"Look at the license plate"—and read out the letters and numbers. Guilt shot through me. Had he never clearly seen those things before and merely acquiesced when we pointed them out?

Ike responded to the concrete and tangible in life in a whole, big-picture way—family walks in the woods, the experience of a soccer team as much in the pizza parlor afterward as on the field during the game. He would describe the texture and smell and colors of things not so much in their particularities as in the way they came together, how they belonged. One of his often-voiced childhood pleas when we would, in his view, overexplain was, "Mom, Dad, don't mess me up with details!"

Nick's vision, in contrast, was keenly accurate, to the smallest detail. He would regularly find the tiniest missing piece to a toy or puzzle. Not yet two, rolling around on the dark blue carpet in the hallway of our home, he had called out, "Look at the ants!" The minuscule creatures, readily apparent to Nick, were hard for us to see even once he had drawn our attention to them. Nick, always hungering for more information, explanation, evidence, details, would frequently approach adults—earnest, index finger on cheek, saying, "Let me ask you a question."

Ike had an appreciation for the whole, and Nick an acute sense and a proclivity for the particular from earliest childhood. As they reached late elementary and early middle school years, their ways of seeing diverged further. Nick, with his intense perception, was immediately aware of the social cues, nuances, and subtleties that go into successful interaction in the war zone of emotions of school and friendships between the ages of eleven and sixteen. Ike yearned for the big picture of friendship and belonging, but he did not know intuitively how to get there. He needed techniques made explicit and practice and coaching, and he had made considerable progress when the new complexities of his illness kicked in at age fourteen.

Since then, the course has often been one of backsliding and regression. Ike means well but often does not perceive how to act on that intent. He values being kind but misses when he is being excessively demanding for what seem muddled purposes. The nuances and complexities of certain relationships escape him; he frequently has crushes on young women who are simply kind to him, not grasping the parameters of courteous behavior. He wants love and caring and romance, and he has memories of times he felt desired, but his sub-scaffolding of learned behaviors and reasoning and judgment to support human relationships is becoming rickety. Life can often seem to be all underpinning, sub-structure, never sufficiently about grand hopes and desires. It can seem all laundry and finances and no looking beyond to a bigger picture, no booming emotions. When I ache for Ike's big wishes and lack of manageable footholds, I try to remember the converse pain many experience.

Ike was comfortable in the ordered, concrete world of his childhood. Participating in a fourth-grade project de-signing note cards, he created a whole world of straight lines—houses and stores lined up on streets, mountains be-hind. It could have been drawn on an Etch A Sketch, every-thing linear and flat and neat.

He was happy as a boy, and he is finding happiness again now at Soltane. It is tempting to skip the years in between but misleading to look only at the destinations without con-sidering the roads. Ike's social difficulties began when many children's do, in late elementary school. At that age, they can arise from real deficits, from differing rates of maturity, from the sorting out from one another that we humans do as we live. I had seen it among my students, and I had read the literature on bullying and ostracizing. Before the illness ap-peared, Ike met with a group of boys and two counselors weekly to receive explicit instruction in the major social behaviors that, if not mastered, could be a death knell to friendship and acceptance. He was making progress, truly "getting it," when the illness and the awkward walk started. For a period of years it was hard to tease out what was actual inability to learn and what was interference from stress, anxiety, or depression about his illness. Looking back now, a slow caving in of his ability to learn is visible.

Ike insisted for years that he was not depressed. He did not like taking medicine and did not stay long on any antidepressant prescribed for him (almost every doctor we saw wrote a prescription for one, without knowing Ike intimately but thinking, This is awful, he *must* need an antidepressant). He was eating and sleeping fine, and for most of the early years of his illness he had two close friends. He has kept in touch with them less and less frequently. One of them has graduated from college. Ike is the only one not driving now. Apart from those two young men, by the middle of eleventh grade, Ike was fairly isolated socially and largely clue-free as to why. The high school counselor had called to report a couple of incidents that were red flags of Ike's inability to understand social interactions. He was making people uncomfortable by standing near them but not participating in their conversations; he would claim that he was speaking. He followed girls that he liked, and he did not see when he was making them feel uncomfortable. We knew it. It did not have to be written across the sky. Ike was perceived by his peers as a "weirdo." An explainable diagnosis would have helped immensely during these years. Without one, we simply tried harder and beat our heads harder against more walls, to no effect.

Nick and Ike were in different schools, but word traveled between the two. Nick, a seventh grader, had to suffer people asking him at school whether he was the "psycho's brother." Nick could see what Ike could not. He could see the mistakes his brother was making, and he hurt for Ike and for himself. Nick took a measure of his own friends by how understanding they were of his brother's increasingly odd behavior. Nick tried to school his brother in the ways of the world, tried to help him develop judgment, taste, an acceptable style. So much effort was expended during these years in things Ike simply could not learn, and so much frustration built up. It would be years before any test would show us incontrovertibly that Ike's brain was atrophying. Then, finally, we would understand more clearly and could piece the past together to make a semblance of sense.

I am not a poet. I share these lines because of their honest expression of the particular agony I have felt in Ike's decline, a sorrow that was surely shaped by our not knowing what was going on with him or why. Only beginning to grasp the bounds of my powerlessness as Ike's mother, I was still understandably where the buck stopped, the one to whom the complaints and reports of "odd behavior" were made, the one who drew the whispers behind hands at parent meetings at his school.

> *From my son's atrophying mind*
> *I hear parroted and parodied*
> *things I have taught, things that*
> *didn't stick*
> *didn't have a chance in hell.*

My own efforts
in him
torture me.

My earnestness
in him
is distorted and
my pain
laughs
at me.

10/22/02

Prank phone calls making fun of Ike were common for a couple of years during high school. Then the ridicule shifted to neglect and invisibility among his peers. Several teachers took extra time with him and showed extra interest. Others were more distant, worn out by what he required. With hindsight, I see that his slide accelerated in eleventh grade. By then he was in committed pursuit of college, as dedicated as he had been with most tasks in his life and seemingly more so as he came to this stage, perhaps sensing that he was losing ground even as he arrived to face the pervasive American middle-class expectation of what comes after high school. We asked whether college was the best next step for Ike, but it was unquestionably what he wanted.

With so many physical setbacks and no sure evidence yet of cognitive decline, and with him being our firstborn and our first child through the college selection process, our reasoning rested on the question—who were we to deny him this dream? He was making the grades, getting the acceptances to the schools of his choice. Who was to say his illness would *not* stop with his walking a little funny and being something of a social cripple—odd, but lovable? See him over some more rough spots, we imagined, hurt for and with him a little more, and we would round the bend to better days. It seemed conceivable.

September 11, 2001, came eight days into Ike's freshman year of college. He called home stunned and worried, as did many college students. Three weeks later we were with him for parents' weekend; his roommate was noticeably absent, gone home, but others in the hallways greeted Ike and us when we passed. Things seemed normal enough. Two weeks later I saw him for his four-day fall break. He was working hard, managing to get around between buildings on the motorized scooter he had needed since August. He studied a lot on his break, got a haircut, and returned to school with seeming pride. Again, things seemed as normal as we had expected college to be for him, given his challenges. Maybe he was really getting it together after all; hope seemed reasonable.

Shortly after midterm, the phone calls began to trickle in. His roommate had told him directly that he hated him, and Ike was stunned, uncomprehending. He could not elaborate on why or what was going on or how he might need to adapt his behavior. I tried to support and reason with him on the phone. I think now, looking back, that those efforts made no sense to him. Unable to differentiate friendliness from pestering, illiterate in reading others, he was repeatedly bumped off Instant Messenger. A phone call to us from the learning support program indicated that he had been missing tutoring sessions, showing up late for class, and not being appropriately deferential or apologetic to the professor about his tardiness—anathema to the compliant, deliberate, conscientious student he had always been. Calls came from him in the middle of the night asking us to solve, long-distance, problems he was having with others in the dorm joyriding on his scooter. Ike must have been experiencing life as insurmountable demands and unfathomable assaults. We did not suspect then what we later learned—that cognitively he was losing ground.

In the second week of November, the call came that a parent was required for an administrative meeting the next day. Backed into a corner by some students, Ike had defended himself by throwing a punch. The administrators were sorry, they knew there were extenuating circumstances, but the school had a no-violence policy. Because of Ike's special physical needs, they were willing to move him to a different living situation. In the course of the night before his father arrived on campus, Ike's confused and anxious actions closed that door to him. His frantic, incoherent interactions with school officials about moving dorms had convinced them that a leave for medical reasons was Ike's best option. They were willing to have him as a day student if we could make living arrangements off-campus.

Noah arrived to find Ike disoriented and confused. College had been beyond him. He had not known how to respect the space of others. He had pestered unknowingly and had become a nuisance. For a combination of reasons, others had had their fun with him. His head was shaved bald; his eyebrows too had been shaved off. His hair, a feature he had prided himself on, had always been thick and full.

This consideration of *the hold of visible things* started with looking and has come to this point of being looked at, of being perceived as other than you perceive yourself, of judgment that is faulty, of mental flexibility that is lacking, of words that refuse to be retrieved, of frustrations that build up with the uncertain sense that things are awry and people are backing you into a corner and telling you they hate you and why don't you go home, when you thought you were in the place to which your whole life had led.

I do not blame the school, and I do not blame the guys. No clear picture existed from which anyone could operate. For a while I blamed myself for having let him go to college, but that led nowhere useful. Any hint there might have been of cognitive decline in the winter and spring of his senior year of high school was reasonably laid at the feet of the stress and anxiety related to the Bence-Jones proteinuria and the subsequent testing for terminal illnesses—amyloidosis and multiple myeloma among them—scary stuff. The first Mayo visit, ruling out these potential killers, ended days before his high school graduation and only weeks before his college orientation in June. Doctors who saw Ike that May and June, to a one, remarked on his "fine mental state" given his physical challenges. Again, who were we to say no to college?

Blaming does not drive the train very far. I hold on to questions of looking and seeing, the minuscule and the big picture, the tiny ants on the carpet and the green carpet of ferns under the trees on an early spring walk with Ike when he was five up Bowman's Hill on the Delaware River.

In the earliest days after Ike's college trauma, retreat was seductive, away from a world where people ridicule by shaving heads and eyebrows and where responses are inarticulate, angry blows. The retreat was not a logical, deductive move, but more an inductive turning to something other. It hurt deeply to have Ike return home in the physical and mental condition in which he came to us. The shaved head was such a dead-on symbol of how much of himself he had lost. I craved George MacDonald's lines *loosen in me the hold of visible things*. I yearned for a different way through *the land of things that swell and seem*.

Looking Again

A GESTURE

Something kind done, something kind said
in spite of everything done and said, in spite
of a soreness of mind, is like being led
to a lawn edged with trees in partial light
where a cloth is spread out for a picnic
—or is it a towel? This is not a picture
but, surprised by sun, put together quick,
a meal of invention startled by nature
into being at all—a startled meal,
arrested on a beach towel, drumsticks,
a half-gone liter of wine—a gift of the real,
an imperfect, conscious attempt to fix
something wrong with something kind, beautiful
because the ragged haste of the gesture is full

of half-creation and suddenly wanting
to do something, since something was wanting.

—MOLLY PEACOCK

Clambering over the fence from seeing as transcendence, I drop into seeing the deliciously mundane. Abstraction has been important with this illness; so have the specific, literal, and tangible.

After Ike's departure from college in the fourth year of his illness, a thorough neuropsychological workup gave us the first proof that, as intelligence is measured, he had lost significant ground. Most of his illness had been chronic, gradual, and even too subtle at times to register as change. Now this stage felt acute, a crisis. The neuropsychological report showed marked cognitive decline in most areas, points off in IQ, substantial loss in speed of processing, retrieval—change across the board, and still no inkling as to why. We were scheduled to see doctors in hematology and neurology again at Mayo that winter. Maybe they would have answers. Maybe the accumulation of symptoms would converge to suggest a new question.

A friend told me about Camphill, an international organization committed since the 1930s to supportive community living for people with disabilities; she had worked in a Camphill community in South Africa. She emphasized the value for Ike of allowing him to continue the separation from home that he had begun by going to college. Ike needed some way to reshape what he was grasping as his failure. I needed to take Nick into account; he was then a junior in high school. I had become aware during Ike's ten weeks at college how little I had heard, much less tended to, Nick in the long years of Ike's illness. The search for a Camphill community for Ike led first to Maple Hill in New Hampshire, and then the next year to Camphill Soltane in Pennsylvania. Both places have been godsends for our family.

Much of the daily stuff of life in Camphill communities is palpable. Maple Hill is a working farm where goats are milked, eggs gathered, sheep raised and shorn, maple trees tapped, bread baked, wood cut to build the fire to warm the house and heat the water, stones stacked to make retaining walls. Everyone takes part in the physical life of the place. Ike's months at Maple Hill demanded a lot of him; much of it he fought against. It took most of the nine months he was there for him to settle in, almost the same time it took for his hair to grow back full and long.

During Ike's time at Maple Hill, concrete experiences of the world became as important to me as the more transcendent had been earlier. I think back of Ike there, kneading bread dough, complaining that it tired his fingers, hurt his hands, that he could not do it even while he was. I think of him snowshoeing in the Special Olympics, complaining, and proud of his medals. As he worked physically, he worked his problems and lost dreams and emotional aches and no-longer-tethered hopes. The Maple Hill community held him and held him accountable in ways Noah and I would not have. They took him as he was. We were still reeling from what he had been and had lost. He was better served by them than by the two of us, and the same is true of Soltane now.

Molly Peacock's poem "A Gesture" is full of tangibility and energies. She gives us a beach towel and drumsticks and *a half-gone liter of wine* along with *soreness of mind* and surprise and invention and startle and *ragged haste* and *half-creation* and sudden wanting. *A gift of the real* and *something kind* bring to mind a friend delivering a jar of bath salts, two people from out of town making time to come and visit, cards sent, notes written, the special mementos, notes, and talismans from students placed in my in-box. These efforts of humans one to the other are often things that can be touched. They come from *wanting / to do something, since something was wanting*. They are *put together quick . . . imperfect*.

Recognizing an effort as imperfect and still worth doing is important in responding to grief—that of others and my own. Sometimes what is called for or what I hear calling up inside me can be strange or quirky, but valuable. The winter of Ike's withdrawal from college, Nick and his friend Meghan came to me with a simple request. Meghan had lost her mom the previous summer in an automobile accident. Meghan and Nick had long been close; in the months since the accident, they had spent many hours of most days together. That Sunday afternoon, they were asking for something unusual but simple. Could they retrieve the empty Martinelli's apple juice jars from the recycling bin in the garage and launch them from Nick's second-floor window onto the blacktop in our backyard?

Why?

They felt the need to break something, they said. Frightening honesty from two sixteen-year-olds. I considered juice jars the least serious of several potential candidates for breakage, and I agreed, stipulating that no one get hurt, including small animals, especially our pets, and that they clean up afterward. They agreed.

Howling with delight at the smashing, the absurdity of it, they intermittently cried and laughed through it. Afterward, sitting talking in the kitchen, we shared the pleasant residue of conspirators in an insanity, which, given our separate and shared losses and grief, struck us as comparatively sane. It was a small, odd, and very physical gesture, with *something kind* in Nick's hatching the idea, in his realizing that it might be something he and Meghan could enjoy and might even need.

That same winter, after Ike's college trauma in November and my final separation from my work at the Atlanta International School, after the neuropsychological evaluation and Ike's move to Maple Hill, after our third weeklong trip to Mayo Clinic, I went to Scotland. I was looking for bleak gray seashores, to defy them to be bleaker and grayer than my heart. I also wanted to spend a few days in the boyhood home of the nineteenth-century writer George MacDonald, whose works I had come to via C. S. Lewis and Auden and Tolkien. I wanted the chance to contemplate at close range the life of one who had lost several children and had continued to write with deep commitment and fullness.

Northeast Scotland in February did not fail to deliver bleakness. Waves sprayed against the dark rocks on which I stood ankle-deep in snow-covered mud and sheep dung. At The Farm in Huntley, I looked up through the window in the roof of MacDonald's boyhood bedroom, the perspective that inspired his characterization of the North Wind, and I slept huddled in the parlor that snowy night, the fire the only heat. The trip itself was a gesture, a putting in place, with *something kind* and determined in the impetus for the trip and in what I experienced there.

Gestures make no claim at being miracles, no pretext at be-all and end-all. They are limited and human. Scotland did not change Ike's struggle. Ike did not win out over the physical challenges of his life at Maple Hill, but they worked small sequential wonders that led to Soltane, where he lives now. Meghan still misses her mom, she and Nick are no longer freshmen, and the three of us smile when we remember the apple juice jars.

Efforts to mend sadness—gestures when something is wanting—feel incomplete. Yet *the ragged haste of the gesture is full / of half-creation* . . . and halfway is not bad, maybe even generous, when considering all that the gesture is made *in spite of.*

Signal Changes

EARLY DARKNESS

Think of it as ink:
an indigo dye descending
between the leaves of the trees
and down to the grasses.

There is no dying of the light—
just the washing of a bowl
and overturning it for night.

When day arrives we must write with
bottled darkness.
In the night we can dream
free messages of light.

—D. PATRICK MILLER

*S*ome poems come and can be received almost effort-
lessly. Some things in life are that way, and I nudge
myself to take notice and not to take for granted. Painful
things at times demand that I sit with them, allow them, and
simply *be* in their presence. At other times the pain prods me
to change it. Do something with me, it seems to say. Put me
somewhere, change me into something you can live with. At
least, show me we've known one another.

Patrick Miller's poem addresses a turning at the crux of
a matter. It offers washing the bowl of day and *overturning it
for night*, changing perceptions to *dream / free messages of
light*. Wordsworth, in *The White Doe of Rylstone*, writes that
through suffering's darkness *(infinite though it seem / And
irremoveable) gracious openings lie*, to be sensed and found. It
is a way of effort and grace, discipline and luck, endurance
and magic. Each can be addressed directly—the darkness,
what Paul Celan calls *the star* and the *thread by which / it
wants to be lowered*.

SPEAK, YOU ALSO

Speak, you also,
speak as the last,
have your say.

Speak—
But keep yes and no unsplit.
And give your say this meaning:
give it the shade.

Give it shade enough,
give it as much
as you know has been dealt out between
midnight and midday and midnight.

Look around:
look how it all leaps alive—
where death is! Alive!
He speaks truly who speaks the shade.

But now shrinks the place where you stand:
Where now, stripped by shade, will you go?
Upward. Grope your way up.
Thinner you grow, less knowable, finer.
Finer: a thread by which
it wants to be lowered, the star:
to float farther down, down below
where it sees itself gleam: in the swell
of wandering words.

—PAUL CELAN
(translated by Michael Hamburger)

With *yes and no unsplit*, the poet requests, *give your say this meaning: / give it the shade*. The *shade* gains ground, strips, and forces growth toward the *less knowable, finer*, recalling the biblical camel through the eye of a needle.

Wanting to see differently, through a received or achieved shift, became strong, at times urgent, for me. I looked for it in tiny moments and snippets of experience.

My first cousin, who is also a very good friend, came with her two daughters and husband to visit me in New York for New Year's. They live in Quebec. Preparing to cross a street, she called to her eleven-year-old daughter, *"Chloé, attends le bonhomme!"*

"Wait for the guy? What guy?" I asked.

"That's what we call the little figure on the light that tells you to walk. That's how he's known in Quebec."

I liked it. I began to think *le bonhomme* each time I looked up and saw the little guy, each time I crossed a street. Naming him brought him to life.

It may be that when there are broken spots in you, the way through will always be altered a little. *Le bonhomme*, the guy, was related to *bonhomie*, good-naturedness. The symbol of the guy walking, the ubiquitous white-light figure, became a statement about normalcy, the way things are intended. Ike with his difficulty walking was not intended, not meant, in the land of good-naturedness, where things are the way they should be. His was the zone of the orange hand, the stop signal. Perhaps I was suffering from midwinter seasonal adjustment disorder to have put such a dismal read on the unassuming little traffic-light figure. I kept thinking; he was hard to avoid.

"The guy" and I now share a special understanding. Like former enemies enjoying a détente, we have been at work on each other. Our truce states that Ike, though he has trouble walking, continues to be *le bonhomme*, the guy, with plenty of good-naturedness—not a norm, but no less intended. An exception.

"Exceptional," *le bonhomme* reminds me at every intersection. There may be others. The little guy negotiated this way reminds me to keep looking.

Lines to Cross

He that lacks time to mourn, lacks time to mend.
Eternity mourns that. 'Tis an ill cure
For life's worst ills, to have no time to feel them.
Where sorrow's held intrusive and turned out,
There wisdom will not enter, nor true power,
Nor aught that dignifies humanity.
—from *Philip van Artevelde*, Part I, Act I, Scene 5,
  by SIR HENRY TAYLOR (1800–1886)

Sparse lines. Stark events. A November appointment. The Babinski reflex. A February hospitalization. Internet searches. A house call.

Thursday, November 13, 1997, the day the neurologist first said "not normal," is a dividing line. It was a rushed after-school appointment in the middle of a million-other-things-to-get-done-before-dinner afternoon in Ike's ninth-grade year. I met his bus after school at the drop-off near our house. Nick, then in seventh grade, was home with Jen, the young woman who helped out in the afternoons so that I could work full-time.

There had been hints before November. That summer, before heading for camp, Ike had complained of shin splints, and the pediatrician had suggested Osgood-Schlatter, a not uncommon knee disorder among teenagers. "Like growing pains, more or less," he said. When Ike came home from camp still complaining, the pediatrician referred him to an orthopedist. Back X-rays ensued, with no significant indication. The orthopedist recommended high-top shoes for ankle support and referred Ike to a neurologist, who found nothing remarkable and scheduled a follow-up in three months.

I had a vague sense that all was not well. Ike had continued to complain about his legs aching, and I had begun to notice black scuff marks when I vacuumed the wooden floor in our front hallway. They were new—his walk was changing. I answered my fears with the reminder that he was at that awkward growth-spurt age when everything can seem for a time a little out of kilter before balancing out. He was my firstborn, and the oldest among his cousins. We had no family benchmarks or points of comparison.

On the way to the doctor's office with Ike, we laughed about the latest antics of his geometry teacher and I listened as he speculated about the school basketball team's prospects. Ike was more curious than anxious about seeing the doctor. We were turning into the parking garage behind the doctor's office building before he mentioned the appointment. It was along the lines of, "So what's up with this appointment, Mom?" He had the confidence born of fourteen years' experience that doctors have answers and make things better.

The pediatric neurologist, Dr. Edward Goldstein, had a reputation as a determined diagnostician. From the diploma on the wall, I saw Hopkins-educated, and when he walked in, I saw serious, dark-haired, about my age, in pajama-like hospital scrubs that did nothing to take the edge off his intensity. His apparent confidence spawned confidence. He spoke very quickly, and I learned in subsequent visits to do likewise and to prepare for our appointments. That first time, we were all innocent.

A hundred years after Joseph Babinski described the reflex that bears his name, the stem end of Dr. Goldstein's hammer stroked across the bottom of Ike's foot and evoked the abnormal response—big toe up, other toes fanning out. Such a small movement brought unmistakable concern to the doctor's face. The hammer end also elicited reflexes from Ike's knees so marked that he came close to kicking the doctor, a scene that would recur numerous times in other exam rooms in the years to follow.

From the dividing line of that appointment, we crossed into a tangling follow-up of tests and scans, fitted in around work, school, activities, and preparations for Ike to move to a new school (he had asked that fall for more academic challenge). Most of the time we were too busy to be anxious. Shoehorning things in had a way of keeping out reflection and worry, or keeping them down to a simmer. MRIs of the brain were taken in early December, near the time of Ike's fifteenth birthday, and of the spine in early January. We would learn later that Dr. Goldstein's first hunch had been a tumor in one of those locations, that the odds for that were higher than for any of the array of rare diseases that might be causing Ike's symptoms. No tumors were found.

A twenty-four-hour hospitalization for a skin-muscle biopsy and a battery of tests were clumped together in early February, a brief hospital stay apparently the best procedure for managing the health insurance paperwork. Reassured that there was a procedure, we took hope. There must have been others, and a plan or an order where we might fit. Concerned, yes, occasionally frantic, but we were not yet adrift.

The Internet had become widely accessible not long before Ike's illness appeared. My self-tutoring in human anatomy and physiology with emphases on neurology and genetics began in earnest. New words and searches—progressive spastic paraparesis, excitatory, inhibitory, neuromuscular junction, hyperreflexia, increased tone. The MRIs did not indicate a cause, and I learned about the process of differential diagnosis, working down a list to diagnose by eliminating. I tracked all the diseases on the list and learned their symptoms and moved on to the next when one was ruled out or a test returned inconclusive. I watched Ike for signs of spreading, worsening, anything new.

The day before his overnight hospitalization, Ike started at his new school, just blocks from our home in Atlanta. He had planned to ride his bike each day. By March, he could no longer ride. His legs lacked the flexibility, and his balance had become unreliable. A neighbor offered to drive Ike every morning. Noah and I both had to leave for work before Ike's school day began. Our need and another's offer of help and the mixed feelings would come again.

That February, our pediatrician telephoned on a Saturday morning and asked if he could come by for a short visit. I was petrified; this was unprecedented. I figured it meant the worst. Dr. Wagner is a handsome bear of a man, kind and intelligent, perceptive and laid-back. What he did that day was a compassionate thing, and it scared the hell out of me. Wanting to speak just to Noah and me, he settled into the square leather chair in our living room and propped his Top-Sider-clad foot across his other knee. His comfort with himself and his warm manner allowed him to get straight to the point without it feeling like the assault that his words surely were. "Ike's got something serious, and there's probably not going to be anything we can do about it. It is likely to get worse. I am here to tell you so that you two can begin to see what's in front of you." This is the gist of what he said to us in the only house call I have ever been party to. What was said back or next is muddled in my memory, but I remember Dr. Wagner's repeated assurances that he was there for us, that we would be largely in the domain of specialists from there forward, but he would be available anytime as a resource, to help us reflect, to negotiate the maze, to be a sounding board.

We were walking him toward the front door, when the conversation turned again. We stopped by the table in the hallway, where I had arranged framed photographs of virtually all of our relatives, a cluttered sort of shrine to family.

"Of course, with these things, if it's hereditary and the inheritance pattern is . . ."

God, no, please don't finish that sentence, don't. Alarms clanged in my head—Nick. That fear had been lurking, I knew; it was not a complete stranger. Doctors, other experts too, probably, can make possibilities seemingly more likely by articulating them. This was beyond bearing right now; it still is.

There might have been some space to mourn that morning, some space to take time, to let go rather than draw in. We did not take it. We closed the door and did not scream or cry or fret. What we did was noiseless. We ratcheted up the anxiety and further set the cast of our exteriors, the stiff upper lip of coping shielding a hunger for privacy and enough distance so that we might still pass as normal. Our engines ran on the energy of the problem-solving mode instinctive to the two of us. We built this precarious fortress and conducted a semblance of living within.

Sir Henry Taylor's lines from his play *Philip van Arte-*

velde are sparse and trimmed. There is little visual richness. The words stand stiffly, meaning what they say with only a twist or two as ornament. They form a clean reflex of a poem with the human touch of a house call. The actors are abstractions—eternity, sorrow, and wisdom. It is a poem about serious business, with the tone of a warning. No-nonsense, its message came to me in a fierce time and suggested that there might be another way, that alongside the busyness and coping and hiding and rational-next-step planning, mourning and sorrow might be admitted.

A faithful friend, poetry works on me. Occasionally with magic, almost always reliably, a poem waits with its message until I turn to it. Taking time for feeling life's worst ills as well as its best joys demands my remembering and re-remembering. Taylor's verse constructs an "if, then"—do it, or else. When I first read these lines, symbolic representations and richly figurative language would have been inaccessible. I was simply too stunned and worn-out after long days of work and nights of online research on rare disorders so that I could advocate intelligently for Ike. I needed this just as Taylor delivered it—straightforward, clear, instructive, and direct.

Taylor's poem uses repetition—*time to mourn . . . time to mend . . . time to feel*. And cushioned, soft rhyme—*mend, them . . . out, power*. Lines with breaks—with periods and commas—slow the reader. In the fourth line there is no break, no comma in *where sorrow's held intrusive and turned out*—no pause through which to enter, the form conveying meaning.

The Scots language has an expression for the gap between the top of the tea and the rim of the cup—the *murning hem*. Loss, sadness, and mourning are expected in life as surely as there is space between the tea and the rim. There, every day, taken for granted, sometimes noted. Perhaps the loss allows the fullness, the part missing keeps the tea in the cup, but for today it is enough simply to perceive the way things are, no compounding it with explanation.

After being read as a directive, Taylor's lines can reconfigure as assurance. Whatever the situation, wherever the attentions or distractions, *Eternity mourns*, the system will groan, the sadness and sorrow will be tended, the *murning hem* minded.

To Bleed

ON TURNING TEN

The whole idea of it makes me feel
like I'm coming down with something,
something worse than any stomach ache
or the headaches I get from reading in bad light—
a kind of measles of the spirit,
a mumps of the psyche,
a disfiguring chicken pox of the soul.

You tell me it is too early to be looking back,
but that is because you have forgotten
the perfect simplicity of being one
and the beautiful complexity introduced by two.
But I can lie on my bed and remember every digit.
At four I was an Arabian wizard.
I could make myself invisible

by drinking a glass of milk a certain way.
At seven I was a soldier, at nine a prince.

But now I am mostly at the window
watching the late afternoon light.
Back then it never fell so solemnly
against the side of my tree house,
and my bicycle never leaned against the garage
as it does today,
all the dark blue speed drained out of it.

This is the beginning of sadness, I say to myself,
as I walk through the universe in my sneakers.
It is time to say good-bye to my imaginary friends,
time to turn the first big number.

It seems only yesterday I used to believe
there was nothing under my skin but light.
If you cut me I would shine.
But now when I fall upon the sidewalks of life,
I skin my knees. I bleed.

—BILLY COLLINS

I am glad I had my boys when I did, that they hit their Age of Opinion on Toys at a time when their father and I could enjoy it too. We found the Muppets and the Ghostbusters easy to love, the Ninja Turtles a little less so, and then we were out of the superhero phase and on to school and sports. For several years, the Ghostbusters were part of the family. Ike and Nick were Peter Venkman and Egon Spengler and Ray Stantz and Winston Zeddmore. I sewed them costumes. They had the official backpacks and ghost traps, and they went about ridding our house and yard and the block of all frightening Sta-Puft giants. The demons were relatively benign. Who could really despise an overgrown marshmallow version of the Michelin mascot? Sure, there were some grotesque ghouls in the movies, but ubiquitous in the post-movie gear was the friendly Casper look-alike on the logo, suggesting that the evil in the world is not so bad. Besides, you can control it. The power and magic of a childhood where you know yourself as ruler of your universe, as the four-year-old Arabian wizard, the seven-year-old soldier, the nine-year-old prince in Billy Collins's "On Turning Ten."

This poem is on turning ten from the vantage point of one who has lived long enough to look back and understand something of the significance. Not long after turning ten,

one of life's major changes—the onset of adolescence—
arrives. For Ike, puberty and illness came simultaneously. A
cruel irony. Just as he was getting a chance to grow tall, to
come alive sexually, the dealer started scooping up the
cards. I need something a little "off" to meet me on this.

Twisted just so from the start, dissonant and ambiguous,
this poem accommodates. I do not have to leave my son,
baggage at the door. From the beginning the boy is *coming
down with something* even as he is growing up. The dialectic, the pulling in opposite directions, is where we live.
The physical and nonphysical, the boy against himself even
in the routine, expected childhood illnesses of measles,
mumps, and chicken pox; the spirit, psyche, and soul are im-
plicated. We feel so often in exile; maybe we are not so
alone here.

When we moved to Atlanta, in 1991, Ike asked for a tree
house and drew a picture of a two-story one he had in mind.
I met a carpenter who was selling his garden benches in a
parking lot one Saturday. Big John, his business card said.
Big John created the tree house in Ike's picture and put it on
posts, wrapped it around and among the trees, too fond of
them to nail it directly to their trunks. A ladder led up to the
tree house, and a second one inside led from the first floor to
the second. Earlier it would have been a Ghostbuster house,
but we were almost out of that phase. Later it would have
been a sad reminder that Ike no longer climbs ladders, but
we moved from that house to one closer to the center of the

city three years before Ike's illness began to show. We drove back past the old house from time to time. Many trees had been taken down, but the tree house was still there, still standing when we left Atlanta after twelve years.

Ike learned to pedal on a small red metal-and-plastic tractor. Because of it he skipped the tricycle, going directly to a bike with training wheels, resenting a little his younger brother's inheriting the tractor. But his legs had become a bit long for it, and he could cover more ground on the bicycle. We moved from our first house to our second to get off a highway and into a neighborhood where the boys could pedal to friends' houses, where we could walk and they could ride after dinner. Family, perceived needs and expectations, have propelled our directions and framed our choices.

Ike stopped riding a bike in March of 1998. His legs had stiffened; he ran into a ditch; it frightened him. He was fifteen when his *bicycle . . . leaned against the garage . . . all the dark blue speed drained out of it*—drained out of it, not him. There is a safety in objects, or a sense of safety, in Ghostbuster costumes and tree houses and bicycles. The speaker in this poem chooses to *walk through the universe in . . . sneakers*, past the *beginning of sadness*—sneakers, not combat boots. I go, as a child, to play—can I?

The poem ends with the simple declaration in the half line *I bleed*. The English word *bless* comes from the Anglo-Saxon *bloedsian*, "to consecrate with blood," but maybe the etymology is a statement of the way things are, not a justification. Maybe it is not that sacrifices buy blessings, but that where sacrifices are, blessings are, a coinciding more than a transaction.

About the same time I read "On Turning Ten," I listened carefully to Elton John's "Blessed." The words are addressed to a yet-to-be-born child: *You'll be blessed, I promise you that, promise you that.* At first, the irony, barbed with sarcasm and flung against my life and Ike's, stung, mocking our hopes and dreams. Yeah, Ike, I really brought you into a blessed life, didn't I? Lousy failure of a parent that I am, lousy failure that I am. I'm so sorry, son. Another parent would have surely done better by you.

Another time I heard in the lyrics the religious boilerplate that we should embrace our suffering and be thankful for it because in it is God's will. You have *got* to be kidding me. Maybe this line of reasoning would work for an illness that belonged to me, but for my son's? That Ike's coming undone, God-ordered, should be received gratefully? Absurd!

But the music kept playing and turned in the middle and turned me. The blade fixed, the lathe turning, the shaping, and again.

Mid-song, the words came in a different way. The voice in "Blessed" could no more guarantee his yet-to-be-born child's happiness than I could take credit or blame for Ike's. The song voiced a wish, and mine too—a declaration, a willing that things be perceived a certain way as much and as often as possible, with allowance for those times when the blessedness cannot be grasped. *I swear you'll be blessed.*

> *You'll be blessed, I promise you that, promise you that*
> *I swear you'll be blessed.*

Yes, Ike, I will see it that way when I can. You already do, more often than I.

A few years before Ike's symptoms appeared, on our way to the North Rim of the Grand Canyon, we stopped to climb on the lava flows of Sunset Crater. Ike fell, and sharp rock and petrified wood stabbed into his knee. A deep gash that would not stop bleeding landed us in the emergency room. Tiger Mom, I went back with Ike to survey the young intern's work as he cleaned and stitched the wound. What was amusing to watch later and to remember now was how Ike milked the injury for all it was worth, and then some, once we arrived at the lodge at the North Rim. He assured us that he would be fine, that we should go on about our day's hike once he was in place, foot elevated, in the main lobby of the lodge. By lunchtime he had made the acquaintance of half the people in the place, and by dinner he knew no strangers and they all knew the story of his injury. As much a story-teller and entertainer as you could expect at his age.

At eleven, he was cut and did shine and did bleed. Now too.

Open to It

_____

Do not hurry
as you walk with grief;
it does not help the journey.

Walk slowly,
pausing often:
do not hurry
as you walk with grief.

Be gentle with the one
who walks with grief.
If it is you
be gentle with yourself.
Swiftly forgive;
walk slowly,
pausing often.

Take time, be gentle
as you walk with grief.

—adapted from GEORGE MACDONALD's *David Elginbrod*

————

Bound—a trouble—
And lives can bear it!
Limit—how deep a bleeding go!
So—many—drops—of vital scarlet—
Deal with the soul
As with Algebra!

Tell it the Ages—to a cypher—
And it will ache—contented—on
Sing—at its pain—as any Workman—
Notching the fall of the Even Sun!

—EMILY DICKINSON, #269

*T*he space grieving requires—the time, walking, pausing, and gentleness in MacDonald's verse—is not
vacuous, but demanding, a null set as complex and troubled
as the *cypher* in Dickinson's verse.

In early April of the fifth year of Ike's illness, he and

I made our way to a snow-covered meadow rimmed with hardwoods on a hill above Bellows Falls, Vermont. To the east from this spot, we could see the black rocks that edge the Connecticut River. A beautiful clearing. The way there was not easy.

The path was open and only slightly uphill, and the woods in early April had little undergrowth to obstruct the way, but there was plenty of snow to challenge Ike, his ability to lift his knees being very limited. His walk had become a pendulum swing. Legs straight through or circling around, knees locked, he plowed the snow in front of him with each dragging, pushing step in the quarter-mile walk to the meadow.

Near the cabin I had found a large stick for him to use. He was thrilled; it seemed to him the sort of walking stick his father's father, Gramps, would use. He fell several times and took me down with him several, and a few times we lay there, the snow having cushioned us against injury, laughing at the spectacle of the two of us sprawled in the snow. Not in a hurry, we had time to move at Ike's pace. Emerging from the woods into the open meadow at the top of the rise, we were in a space not totally exposed, the trees hugging the meadow's rim, framing it. Ike chose to sit on a stump near the edge of the woods. I ran on out into the middle of the open field, in snow untouched save for a few deer tracks. I clowned, made him laugh.

No cakewalk. But reached, we found room to see.

The challenges in the way to the meadow for me were

different from Ike's. I was in a whiteout snowstorm of anxiety following Ike's traumatic college experience and the neurological assessment that had found significant cognitive loss. I could not fathom the dimensions of the storm, much less feel a way through. Maple Hill in New Hampshire where Ike had been living since early December closed for two weeks in the spring. I needed to be near Keene to take care of Ike so that he could continue with the one college course in which he was enrolled. It was a time of many mixed signals. Working hard, he had garnered the sympathy of the teacher and yearned to belong with the students. His slipping was apparent. His thinking was often illogical, disjointed, his recall of material he read full of holes.

His decline in these days was wicked. It would masquerade as purely physical only to ambush me—and perhaps Ike (his awareness of things and the extent to which things bothered him were often difficult to discern). He would make a convincing case for my driving him hours in the dark and snow to hear an evening speaker on a topic that interested him, only to be unable to express his thoughts about it afterward. One evening, cleaning up after dinner, he put the leftover green salad in the cabinet. When I questioned him about it, he did not see the mistake. When I reminded him that salad goes in the refrigerator, no light went on. Conversations ranged from odd to bizarre to agonizing and did not arrive at resolutions that Ike could hold on to, nor at a clearer picture of himself.

His homework took him hours. I estimated it at about

four times what the instructor had expected most students would spend. Logging on to the university's library system confused Ike. It became my daily job to dial in and go through the connection protocol for him. Troubleshooting and problem solving were handed back to me. He could not retain the solutions.

At a point earlier, one doctor had briefly considered the possibility that Ike's cognitive situation was constant and only appeared progressive as the school supports for him fell away and the challenges of adulthood mounted. We had looked around for a while in the domain of Asperger's syndrome, and Ike very much wanted me to meet a psychology professor at Keene State whom he had come to know, a man with an academic interest in Asperger's syndrome. I went to meet him one day while Ike was in class. The professor pulled in a colleague; they were both interested in Ike's story. Both kind, they were accustomed in their field to "cases"; they said Ike's was complex, that he was "multi-problemed." Interest and sympathy and the knowledge that they had extended these to Ike were what they could offer me. It would be my job to hold Ike steady until he could see, with time, that that was the end of the story with these teachers and at that college too. A space unfilled, a cycle not finished.

For months Ike desperately wanted to go back to college full-time. He refused to see anything that was happening as other than "mistakes" he had made. Imagine his un-bounded, unfounded guilt, his vast sense of inadequacy. I now try to see Ike's raw wishes served up, his occasional rants as feelings to cradle and contain until they can be let go. I was then only beginning to understand the early stages of his cognitive loss. It was, to that point, the time of his greatest scream.

The clearings that opened for us during our time in Vermont were not planned. I cannot claim wisdom of foresight, only chronicling of experience. There were few other doors left to open. A friend would help me see many months later the value of full awareness of the emptiness, and another would remind me again years later.

If not other snowstorms, there had been other fogs, and they did not always lead to openings—fogs in the course of Ike's illness that I had wanted to call optimism, but looking back, I know they were denial. In these fogs we had marched on, supported him in school, kept working full-time ourselves, adding on physical therapists and lap swimming and back specialists, taking things in stride as his stride was faltering. I cannot envision another way his father and I would have done it. "Determined" had been a big part of my nature, my husband's too. We were determined, of course, to get to the bottom of Ike's health issues, but we were also determined to keep the jobs we found meaningful and felt fortunate to have, and we were determined to help Ike reach his own goals.

If it looked different from the outside, if it looked as if we were pushing rather than supporting him, no one broke through the fog to tell us. We knew he was challenged at school, but he had always been a hard worker, and little had come easily to him. Since fourth grade we had known that Ike had some learning disabilities, and we had followed up with the recommended school placements and tutors, along with a measure of our own common sense. All living, with or without challenges such as Ike's, occurs in a morass of unknowns. We told ourselves that ours was just a bit more convoluted and more often colored by a sense of impending bad news.

The decision to move from Atlanta in the sixth year of Ike's illness and the process of packing brought the opening of a discovery. I was sorting through piles of things, deciding what to keep, what to pitch, how to order them. On the floor in the extra room I laid out years' worth of both boys' school papers and, in the midst of it, Ike's writing from ninth grade forward. There it was—the biggest slip, most apparent in the second half of eleventh grade. There was the proof, the documentation of reasoning increasingly riddled with holes, compositions going from carefully constructed and meaningful to more confused and disjointed, with small strands of pseudo-reasoning, trailing off.

Openings in this illness and sadness have shown up unexpectedly, making room for attention and intention.

In Eudora Welty's *The Optimist's Daughter*, Laurel, sitting in the waiting room as her daddy is dying, gives others waiting "the wide berth of her desolation." Desolation demands a wide berth and brings a seeing that eludes me in crowded busyness. Anne Morrow Lindbergh, who was forced to grieve her son's death publicly, given her husband's celebrity and the public attention to the kidnapping, wrote, "A tree has significance if one sees it against the empty face of the sky. A note in music gains significance from the silences on either side." A wide berth does not mean shut down, but a sometimes radical change in perspective, a different slant, a place of sharp seeing.

Space to work, demanding mindfulness, like the meadow exposed held in context. The word *cypher* in Emily Dickinson's poem leads in so many directions. Math and measurement. Zero, nonentity, any Arabic numeral, any character, hieroglyph, or symbol, a secret code, the interweaving of letters as in a monogram, the sounding of an organ pipe without pressure on the key. Even when it stands for nothing, *cypher* conveys meaning and holds place. And that meaning can be written or sounded, literal or symbolic, obscured or fully elaborated. A bounded, resounding, everyday space. A *cypher*. The reassuring confines of a zero, o. The effortless humming of a life even when no music is being asked of it. The reliable regularity of time ticking off.

In the space, the cypher, the zero, *will ache— contented—on.*

Sifting Questions

How long, O Lord, must I call for
help,
but you do not listen?
. . . you do not save?
Why do you make me look at injustice?
Why do you tolerate wrong?

—from Habakkuk 1:2–3

A n early response to the news that things with Ike were "definitely not normal" was to look for meaning, consolation, and energy perhaps, in Scripture. The Bible had been a major part of my upbringing. When I was a child, my family read devotions every morning at the breakfast table and worshipped at church on Sundays. Both of my sons were baptized in a Presbyterian church, but I have not been as structured and diligent with them in things religious as my parents were with me. Personally I have been serially and cyclically active, reluctant, neglectful, disinterested, and absent with regard to formal religion. Recently I told a friend that for the most part God has convinced me she's there, but not always that we should be speaking. When I reread that last sentence even now, I want to underline and qualify the *for the most part.*

What I knew for sure was that when Ike's illness cut into our lives, piety and professed quick fixes alternately appalled me and left me cold. I could listen only to those who themselves had experienced pain. When things were at their worst, proof of genuine suffering was my prerequisite for giving attention.

I craved words that laid it out without placating, that voiced the devastation without pretense of cheap consolation. The pain was costly; it seemed to make sense that any supposed fix would have to be. I hurt like hell, and if a poem could put words to that, I needed that poem. I needed just to know that another someone had experienced something with a shape or sound or smell or texture or hue like my sorrow, the deep-to-the-soul uncertainty, the hunger I suspected might never be satisfied.

Shock. What do you mean, Fleshy Boy is "not normal"? Noah and I had called him Fleshy Boy in his first months just between ourselves, because that was what he was—

fleshy, plump, cuddly, substantial. His essence was not bony, apart from a very hard head, which could assuredly inflict pain if a head bob caught the one holding him unawares. With his fleshiness came a generally sunny disposition. He was an "easy baby." How could this darkness come into a place all had tended so carefully to make bright? *How long . . . must I call . . . / but you do not listen? / . . . Why do you make me look at injustice? / Why do you tolerate wrong?*

From the main teachings of religions, devout people of many faiths find all they need to handle suffering. My faith (pairing those words seems to me a bit presumptuous) is perhaps too nascent or immature, or maybe I get in its way. I needed to look also in places other than Scripture. Lines from Eliot's "East Coker" came back to me in ways perhaps other than the poet's intent; they would not leave me alone.

It was not (to start again) what one expected.
   . . .

      Had they deceived us
or deceived themselves, the quiet-voiced elders
Bequeathing us merely a receipt for deceit?
The serenity only a deliberate hebetude,
The wisdom only the knowledge of dead secrets
Useless in the darkness into which they peered
Or from which they turned their eyes . . .

I said to my soul, be still, and wait without hope
For hope would be hope for the wrong thing; wait
    without love
For love would be love of the wrong thing; there is yet
    faith
But the faith and the love and the hope are all in the
    waiting.
Wait without thought, for you are not ready for
    thought:
So the darkness shall be the light, and the stillness the
    dancing

> —from "East Coker," *Four Quartets*,
> by T. S. ELIOT

He had more questions and a strategy—*wait without hope . . . without love . . . without thought* because . . . *the faith and the love and the hope are all in the waiting*. The questions of the poet add to the prophet's. What do you mean? How can it be? Why? I heard in these voices my own pleas and my own attempts at sense-making. Habakkuk was taking his grief directly to the source and pleading, Hey, some accountability here, please. I needed Habakkuk's questions. How do you get away with this, God? What's the deal here? I read these lines from Habakkuk again and again, as well as Eliot's questioning whether we had been deceived by the perhaps self-deceived *quiet-voiced elders*.

I could not proceed to God's reply to Habakkuk nor to

Habakkuk's statement of faith at the end of the tiny book. I was not ready. Eliot's lines suggest that inside the infinitive "to wait" lie the infinitudes of faith and love and hope. Eight years into Ike's illness, there is still a truth to the words that *hope would be hope for the wrong thing; . . . love would be love of the wrong thing;* and there are still times when I am *not ready for thought.* But at least these lines gave me a place from which to say "O Lord," and addressing a god is a stance I have not always been able to assume.

Well Wishers

THE WELL OF GRIEF

Those who will not slip beneath
the still surface on the well of grief

Turning down through its black water
to the place we cannot breathe

will never know the source from which we drink,
the secret water, cold and clear,

nor find in the darkness glimmering
the small round coins
thrown by those who wished for something else.

—DAVID WHYTE

Not long ago, I was in a small town, new to me, where one of the centers of activity is a delightful knitting store. Even if it were just a yarn shop, it would not be just a yarn shop, the stock lush in texture and hue, a feast for the fingers, a gallery to be squished, to be taken in here and here and here, up close and stepping back. But it is a knitting store where people do knit—there, not at home, at least for a few hours of the day—there where they can knit together and, oh yeah, by the way, share their lives. It was in this setting that Beth said, "Everyone says he's getting so much better, but I know he's not." This was how she brought up the heartbreak of her husband's accident. In a December snow and ice storm, a tree had fallen on his car. He had suffered serious brain injury. She did not begin with the horrible details of the accident, nor with a lament, however justified, about his plight or hers. What was breaking her heart that particular bright January afternoon was that she was alone in clearly seeing his condition. Alone, left there with the best intentions of well-wishers.

Wells were on the periphery of my growing up. Sunday afternoons for most of my childhood and adolescence we visited both sets of grandparents. Each had a well on their property. The wells seemed ordinary, not magical wishing wells. I remember the one at Granddaddy's mainly as a potential danger, deep and dark, its makeshift cover an irregular piece of scrap metal held in place by spare bricks. The sort of place you could really get hurt falling down into.

We made more wishes on coins thrown into fountains than into wells. When Ike was twelve, he threw coins into the Trevi Fountain. Eleven of us were spending a month in rented flats in the tiny Tuscan village of Fonterutoli, with women cutting lavender on the hillsides in the early morning, lemon trees rising above the garden walls, and wine being bottled in the space beneath us, where it had been bottled for five centuries. Ike and Nick and three of their cousins splashed in what they were convinced was the world's coldest swimming pool. The vineyard workers were amused by our amusements. We accompanied my father over battlefields where he had fought in World War II. On our way home, we went through Rome. We threw lire and nickels in the Trevi Fountain. We all wanted to return.

"He's not really any worse," a friend would say, hoping to console.

"He looks like he's doing well. He's really doing well," another would say. What she was saying was that "it" is not so bad from her perspective, while leaving us to "it," reminding us that "it" was Ike's, ours—not hers. Alienation had not been her intention. More likely her desire that it be true, or her fear, or her genuine concern had caused her to speak.

Those Who Mean Well. Well-wishers.

People in pain are often handed platitudes alongside the best intentions. In the face of searing pain and gaping loss, much can seem flat, stale.

How much I need someone to know that the well is deep, that its substance is grief, that the water we drink is black, that when I am down there, I cannot breathe, and that I am screaming, screaming that I had wanted something else.

A *glimmering*. In the poem. Musicians call it glissando—rapidly executed, a sliding. David Whyte does it with the single word, *glimmering*. The poem hinges on this word. The *glimmering* glissando slides on to suggest that there may be bright things in the darkness, deep down.

A well springs from groundwater. Groundwater connects in the water cycle to rain, dew, the sea. At the bottom of the well is connection.

The wishes of the well-wishers, incomplete and imperfect, come from deep springs. They strain upward through layers of many-hued emotions and motivations. Each is an ultimately human expression, flawed, inadequate, incomplete. The groundwater, our commonality, may be in the wishing.

Vividly Inarticulate

_____

TANTRUM

A child's cry out in the street, not of pain or fear,
rather one of those vividly inarticulate
yet perfectly expressive trumpet thumps of indignation:
something wished for has been denied,
something wanted now delayed.

So useful it would be to carry that preemptive howl
always with you; all the functions it performs,
its equivalents in words are so unwieldy,
take up so much emotive time,
entail such muffling, qualifying, attenuation.

And in our cries out to the cosmos, our exasperation
with imperfection, our theodicies, betrayed ideals:
to keep that rocky core of rage within one's rage

with which to blame, confront, accuse, bewail
all that needs retaliation for our absurdly thwarted
   wants.

                         —C. K. WILLIAMS

C ollecting is a part of many childhoods: seashells, rocks, stamps, coins, bottle caps, ticket stubs, caps, cards of all sorts—baseball cards, postcards. Some collections develop into lifelong hobbies and sources of much pleasure; others gather little interest but accumulate lots of stuff until the next cleaning or the next move, space and tolerance levels dictating.

My sons and I have a quirky little collection. Not planned, it happened. The items are from vacations, from places where we found ourselves with time to notice and one of us would stop and reach down and pick up something that seemed to want to be kept. And I have kept them, in clear little film cylinders, their origins scribbled in marker on the outside. Some are seashells, and a few are from places I went alone. Three are rocks from places we walked together.

The largest, the length of my thumb, is a rusty iron volcanic rock, more red on one side, more gray-black on the other, with jagged edges, flat. As I hold it now, it looks as though it would be a good skipping stone, but the place from which it was retrieved was no quiet pond or lazy river conducive to skipping. Several times in the nineties we took the boys to Aruba, far enough south in the Caribbean to be predictably warm and below the usual hurricane belt. The rock is from the eastern, unsheltered side of the desert island, where the sea slams hard. The view there is sharp contrasts, deep red rock, dark blue sea, dry soil with sparse vegetation, constant blazing sun. The rock has given way here and there to the sea's sculpting. As with many islands, there is a "natural bridge," the tourist attraction that brings the bus out to this point—that and the lighthouse. The windward side of the island is my favorite, where the surf pounds, away from the development of the leeward side, with its clean, sheltered white sand. On the windward side, I cannot swim; I can only stand and watch and witness the grandeur. And I can pick up a rock and remember that a volcano threw it out and made this island, surrounded by a sea that pounds at it and wears it away.

I hold this rock in my hand and think of the line in C. K. Williams's poem, *that rocky core of rage within one's rage*. I know that when Ike knelt and picked it up and handed it to me, he could kneel and could stand back up by himself without a cane or a supportive arm. And that neither he nor I had any idea of the shipwreck that was to come.

The second rock is from Sunset Crater, another volcano, thousands of miles northwest of Aruba, in Arizona. Another pre-illness find, this one is tiny, not much bigger than an eraser on the end of a pencil, rather cube shaped, and pumicelike, with the same shades of red and black as the Aruba rock. A fragment, this little rock seems more a morsel than a thing unto itself. It is hard to find power or rage, anything volcanic, in this small piece. What is easy to see on close examination is the reason for the rock's surprising lightness—its pervasive holes. Thrown violently from the inner core and cooled quickly, this rock is lots of tiny spaces, not continuous solid surface. The gas and the solid interspersed, interdependent, adhering to one another. Some of the holes are deep, others only divots, no two alike. Dialectics and competing tendencies. My small rock of opposites from Arizona.

The third rock is smooth. Of the three, it is the prettiest. Between the other two in size, it is comparable in length to the first joint of my thumb. Pleasant to the touch, the rock is a cross section, with a nondescript beige-ish outer skin and an intriguing interior of lovely yellows of varying intensity. It is metamorphic, probably from sediment. Ike picked it up on the seashore in Normandy in 1999.

At sixteen, Ike consented reluctantly to travel outside of the United States for the first time since becoming sick. Staying close to home had become important to him. The four of us were together in France for two weeks. Paris was hard for Ike. Too many stairs, he said. Looking back from his current level of disability, it is hard to imagine that we undertook it, but he was much more mobile then, needing neither a cane nor a scooter. He already had trouble descending but not yet so much difficulty ascending stairs. He seemed in fact to do better with more movement; long periods of sitting were a nemesis. Still, it was a hard time for Ike and for all of us straining to come to grips with desires to do and go and see and with the frustrations of limitations inadequately understood and incompletely expressed.

Normandy by comparison was an unmitigated pleasure for Ike; he basked in the experience. There was the water, the Channel, the beauty, the quiet. Walking was on flatter ground with fewer people around. We stayed at Grandcamp-Maisy, at a hotel on the water with a staff that treated us like family. We shared an enormous tureen of mussels at one end of the dining room and lingered long over the meal, watching the sun set over the Channel. By the time we left, the waiters and waitresses were enjoying their own meal together at the other end of the room. The feeling of family was key to Ike's enjoyment. That and the history of Pointe du Hoc, just to the east, not in the detail-driven way his brother experienced the history, but in his own holistic, Ike sort of way.

He loved Normandy, and we began to look for an excuse to return. In his tenth-grade year, Ike was impressed by a favorite teacher's enthusiastic introduction to the works of Alexis de Tocqueville. Googling him led to a Tocqueville family home in Normandy that could be rented and would accommodate nine. The next summer, thirteen of us spent a week there. Our family shared the Tocqueville home with my older brother's family. My younger brother and his children stayed nearby.

When I hold this rock from the shore in Normandy and remember those times together, it is hard to rage. This rock, metamorphic, has been changed. Ike's sadness has cut into our family, but it has also refashioned us and at times brought us together.

Rocks are underrated, overlooked, assumed to be static, unchanging. They are often clichés of strength. They are stacked in remembrance, in commemoration. In the Old Testament, Samuel sets one up and calls it Ebenezer: "Thus far the Lord has helped us" (I Samuel 7:12). A hymn I remember from my youth builds on this.

> *Here I raise my Ebenezer*
> *Hither by thy help I'm come*

When the situation looks bleakest, I want to scream back, "If this is where your help has brought me, thanks, but no thanks. Leave me the hell alone!"

The rock from Normandy has been pushed and changed and compacted by great pressures into something else. The rock from the windy side of Aruba pounds with the terrifying power of the volcanoes and the sea and the rage that wants to be seized and shouted out, however inarticulately. The tiny fragment of Arizona pulls together opposites, puts things across differently from what might be expected.

The poem's ending settles down around the word *thwarted*. Thwart is from a family of words that gives rise to transverse, crosspiece, oblique, cross-grained. It is not being stopped entirely, but being thrown askew. Things still get through, but at an odd angle, "athwart." In its nautical usages, athwart distinguishes the direction side to side from fore and aft. One ship may lie athwart the course of another. In *thwarted wants* is the possibility of moving. Rather than a dead standstill is the possibility of going by another way.

Courage? Yes

---

love is a place

love is a place
& through this place of
love move
(with brightness of peace)
all places

yes is a world
& in this world of
yes live
(skilfully curled)
all worlds

—E. E. CUMMINGS

When Ike left for college in the fall of 2001 and I had taken a leave from teaching and my mornings were no longer bustling with my own busyness, I was sitting in the kitchen one morning listening to Nick's getting up, showering, and getting dressed sounds. Just listening to Nick. I realized that for years I had not listened to Nick's sounds. My ear had been trained to sounds of Ike falling, calling out, needing something. I had let Nick slide.

For the next two months I focused on Nick front and center and talked about my worries about Ike a little less. Nick is energetic, his personality and bright mind as irrepressible as his unruly reddish hair. He is a *yes* guy— not an obsequious "yes," but eagerly open and ready for the next thing. He is big on following his heart and big on questioning.

Almost every year in grades seven through twelve, a major English paper for Nick had turned into a piece about his brother. When Ike left for college, Nick's paper ended where he hoped the story would—in his brother's victory over the unknown illness. When the call came that Ike would need to take a leave from college, I refrained from telling Nick for several days, biding time until the weekend, going over the words in my head, rehearsing how to break the news to him. When Noah called to say that he and Ike were within hours of home, in the U-Haul with all of his stuff, I tried to talk to Nick about what had happened. He fell on the kitchen floor and sobbed. I sat down next to him and held his head in my lap.

A year later Nick lay flat out on the same kitchen floor, this time jubilant.

"Yes. Yes." I heard from upstairs. He had phoned the college admissions office and learned that he had been accepted. By the time I reached the kitchen, he was lying on his back on the floor, his eyes moist.

"Finally," he said. "Vindication." Laying claim.

I had heard the admonitions and read the articles about the overlooked sibling of the chronically or terminally ill. I thought I had been paying particular attention, and Nick had been fairly good all along at laying claim to things he felt were rightfully his. In 1998, close on our first inklings of Ike's illness, Nick stepped forward and informed us that we still had to do things as a family, we could not just stop everything while we worried and waited. Our twelve-year-old, challenging us to regroup. That March, Nick accompanied his father on the business-and-pleasure trip to Mexico that the four of us had planned to take together. I stayed home with Ike, who was newly resistant to travel, what with the physical changes he was experiencing.

Nick thrives on adventure; being with him in the midst of it is great fun. The summer Nick was fourteen, he and I went ahead to Paris a week before Noah and Ike. Nick delighted in his ability to communicate in French; he loved running by himself to the grocer's, a block away, knowing that he could manage to get what was needed, speak the language, pay in the foreign currency. Each time he returned, he was more full of energy, more alive. When Noah and Ike arrived the next week and the energy shifted to accommodating Ike, Nick still generated energy. He has often been for me the courage encouraging.

As small boys, Ike and Nick played together well, almost always, when it was just the two of them. I did not have to force or impose or be didactic; they just got along—Isaac, the older, gentler; Nick, the firebrand, yet looking up to his brother, sensing perhaps at a young age that his fights in life would be with others.

> *What is our innocence,*
> *what is our guilt? All are*
> *naked, none is safe. And whence*
> *is courage: the unanswered question,*
> *the resolute doubt,—*
> *dumbly calling, deafly listening—that*
> *in misfortune, even death,*
> *encourages others*
> *and in its defeat, stirs*
>
> *the soul to be strong?*

—from "What Are Years?"
by MARIANNE MOORE

As a parent, it is difficult to admit with Marianne Moore that *none is safe* where my children are concerned. Some things make the point vividly; some only hint. One March, years before Ike's illness, we had a week out of school. At dawn on a Sunday we awoke the boys, popped baseball caps on the two of them, and headed for the airport, then to Florida for baseball spring training, a dream vacation come true for Noah and the boys. On board, I must have had the complacent look of a parent fulfilling her family's desires.

We were at who knows what altitude—twenty, twenty-five thousand feet—cruising the moderate distance between Atlanta and West Palm Beach. The plane started shaking and bouncing. I was seated between the two boys, who were then eight and ten. Noah was across the aisle.

"What is that, Mom? What's happening?" Nick asked, his voice pitched a bit high.

"Oh, don't worry. It's okay," I said, and I put my arms around the two of them and looked straight ahead. I knew Nick would see the fear in my eyes.

As the plane's shaking and bouncing continued, harder and more sustained than I could recall experiencing, I knew that there was absolutely nothing I could do but cover my illusions of control with illusions of calm. Illusions they would certainly be. I was truly, keenly afraid for my sons, for whom I was responsible, for whom I had made the decision to get on the plane that morning.

So many times through the years, I had thought I was keeping them safe. In fact, that had rarely been in my power, and the extent to which I could protect them was shrinking exponentially each year. No longer were they toddlers reaching to explore the dials on the old gas stove. As surely as the plane was bumping and rattling in the clear-air turbulence, Ike and Nick were flying away in their lives beyond any ability of mine for safeguarding. As the plane calmed, I did; the turbulence passed. We landed, and the panic-provoked realization of powerlessness thinned out and was as easily discarded as my boarding pass. A residue remained, a muffled, tucked-away awareness that there would be more frightening moments in my sons' lives, things more sustained and wrenching than airplane turbulence, things that would rattle and shake with no apparent cause and no near-term end.

When the boys were three and five years old, two incidents happened back-to-back; each was an experience in loss of something precious at the time. Each boy had a few bad dreams about the lost thing, fretting and worrying. Looking back, the losses seem small, silly almost; they did not to the boys at the time. The first one happened to Ike. He dropped a tiny paintbrush he had been using down the bathroom sink drain when he was washing it. With no possibility of retrieval, Ike fretted over "the little paintbrush down there in the dark . . . lost!" Not twenty-four hours later, Nick, stepping off the stool on which he stood to use the toilet, doing things with his usual bravado and flair, flicked his favorite red and yellow clown washcloth from the towel bar into the air. The toilet lid still up, the toilet flushing, the washcloth airborne, Nick batted the cloth, again as usual, toward the sink, where he would move next to continue his cleanup for bed. The cloth landed in the flushing toilet, and the clown was down the drain, much as the paintbrush had been the day before. Nick was stunned, motionless. Wide-eyed and openmouthed for ten or fifteen seconds, he broke into shrieks of disbelief followed by sobs. To think, Yellow Clown was gone forever. Each of these was a small loss; new paintbrushes and washcloths with other appealing characters could be found. What struck me was each boy's immediate sense of loss and my own instantaneous desire to fix it. Both seemed to flood in before thought. Stepping back and letting be, letting grow, especially amid sadness, is not instinctual; it requires effort.

I have a small collection of four pictures of the two boys. I had discovered, in a summer's sorting of photographs accumulated through the years, that in significant ones I was often taking pictures of Ike and Nick together from behind. There they were, toddling along at ages three and five up the hill outside of Cabot, Vermont, and then at eleven and thirteen wading through the waist-high grass beneath the silver-green leaves of the olive grove winding up to the town of Vinci, in Tuscany. In these two, there is no sign of Ike's illness. Then a year or two later, there was Ike, his arm draped over Nick's shoulder, the two of them making their way up a gentle incline at the Desert Museum outside Tucson. In the most recent picture, the boys, fifteen and seventeen, are walking late in the day in the loggia at the Palais Royal in Paris. In these last two, Ike's back and legs akimbo, the illness has begun.

It is a perspective I am trying to hold on to—this letting go. Stepping back, observing my two sons, I can see Nick continue to claim his own life, to vindicate, to answer life *yes*, and, in that, to love his brother. I see Ike claiming his life, in part by pulling his brother's to himself, delighting in Nick's every tale, devouring his every experience, fretting about him at times, curling into his brother's *yes* world. The *yes* is not an all-the-time done deal; it is not perfection. It is an alternative and a choice.

> *You are always the member of a team,*
> *Accompanied by a question—*
> . . .
>
>   *Am I a yes*
> *To be posed in the face of a negative alternative?*
> *Or has the sky taken away from me its ultimate guess*
> *About how probably everything is going to be*
> *   eventually terrible*
> *Which is something we knew all along, being modified*
> *   by a yes*
> *When what we want is obvious but has a brilliantly*
> *   shining trail*
> *Of stars. Or are those asterisks? Yes.*
> . . .

I love your development
From the answer to a simple query to a state of peace
That has the world by the throat . . .

—from "To 'Yes' "
by KENNETH KOCH

Bearing Things

PRAYER

My prayers, my God, flow from what I am not;
I think thy answers make me what I am.
Like weary waves thought follows upon thought,
But the still depth beneath is all thine own,
And there thou mov'st in paths to us unknown.

—GEORGE MACDONALD

FRATERNITY

I ask not how thy suffering came,
Or if by sin, or if by shame,
Or if by Fate's capricious rulings;
*   To my large pity all's the same.*

Come close and lean against a heart
Eaten by pain and stung by smart;
It is enough if thou hast suffered,—
  Brother or sister then thou art.

We will not speak of what we know,
Rehearse the pang, nor count the throe,
Nor ask what agony admitted
  Thee to the Brotherhood of woe.

But in our anguish-darkened land
Let us draw close, and clasp the hand;
Our whispered password holds assuagement,—
  The solemn "Yea, I understand!"

—ANNE REEVE ALDRICH

*I*t seemed I was holding my sorrows in front of me like a folded flag in a graveside ritual, leaning forward, kneeling to put them in a hallowed place where they might be understood or where they could join with all there that is not.

On my first 9/11 living in New York, the second anniversary of the World Trade Center attacks, I was restless all day. Somehow I needed to share in the grief, yet I had not earned that precious right. I had not been hurt enough, not personally affected, and those who had been seemed very set apart, deserving ultimate care and respect.

Watching the city come into view from the train on my way home from seeing Ike's doctor in Philadelphia, watching the lights as I crossed the desolate area in New Jersey right before the train moves into the pitch-black tunnel that signals passengers to start putting on their coats, collecting their things, the word *violence* came to me—the violence that had been done on 9/11—and the word *violate* and the French verb *violer*, "to steal." Much was stolen that day from that place in lower Manhattan. The word *bereavement* stems from roots of deprivation, from things taken away.

When something is stolen, it is natural to take stock of what has not been. When we were quiet four times on September 11, 2003, four moments of silence, one for each tower being hit, one for each tower falling, some things did not go silent, things that seemed not to heed the commemoration—horns, sirens, birds, babies, my friend on the park bench. Complete silence and absolute vacuums are rare. Perhaps they exist only in theory. Perhaps there is a generative power in emptied-ness, vacancy, engines that start when all is stripped down and cleared away, in times of wandering in the wilderness, exile, desertion, being disowned. Oliver Sacks, in *A Leg to Stand On*, quotes the verse from John Donne that was helpful to him in the quiescence of his personal confrontation with injury and debility.

> *For his art did expresse*
> *A quintessence even from nothingnesse,*

From dull privations, and lean emptinesse,
He ruin'd me, and I am rebegot,
Of Absence, Darknesse, Death; things which are not.

—from "A Nocturnal upon St. Lucy's Day"
by JOHN DONNE

At this point of *lean emptinesse*, the human rush to fill is the greatest—for the person experiencing the pain or grief, and for the witness, the caring bystander. In this presence of nearly overwhelming absence, I am inclined to rush another's grief, sometimes ironically, selfishly, for my own comfort. I rush to say the positive thing, to try to make sense, to smooth over, perhaps with good intentions but at the risk of alienating even further the person grieving. When others rush me in this way, I hurt, feeling not wronged as much as wrong. What is wrong with me if I do not see things quite as neatly patched up and explained as my friend says they are? How hard it is when I am in that horrible aching place, or when I see others in it, to stand in place in need, to wait for Donne's *rebegot*.

How can I dwell in full view of Ike's diminished capacities, just dwell? How can anyone who looks at the blank air that the World Trade Center towers once filled, anyone who lost someone there, dwell in the presence of *things which are not*? It boggles the mind. Unhealed wounds and unresolved suffering are difficult to grasp long term.

Unsought, two tensions tug in different directions. One

tension pulls me to stand squarely in front of the precise texture of the losses—Ike's, mine, ours. The other pulls me to a place where it is impossible to see only that. In the apparent unmoving, pulls and tensions and forces are at sway, movement implicit in the stillness, beneath it to hold it up, and in it, its essence. Perhaps these tensions arise from the *nothingnesse* to which Donne refers, from the place where prayers, spoken and silent, come—*from what I am not*. In George MacDonald's "Prayer," energy flows on the surface in waves of thought, *weary*, meted out, relentlessly, repeatedly, and in the still depth, the underlying vibrato.

HIS STILLNESS

*The doctor said to my father, "You asked me
to tell you when nothing more could be done.
That's what I'm telling you now." My father
sat quite still, as he always did,
especially not moving his eyes. I had thought
he would rave if he understood he would die,
wave his arms and cry out. He sat up,
thin, and clean, in his clean gown,
like a holy man. The doctor said,
"There are things we can do which might give you time,
but we cannot cure you." My father said,
"Thank you." And he sat, motionless, alone,
with the dignity of a foreign leader.
I sat beside him. This was my father.*

He had known he was mortal. I had feared they would have
to tie him down. I had not remembered
he had always held still and kept silent to bear things,
the liquor a way to keep still. I had not
known him. My father had dignity. At the
end of his life his life began
to wake in me.

—SHARON OLDS

In her poem, Sharon Olds gives us the stillness of her father's dying, his . . . *Absence, Darknesse, Death* . . . in Donne's words; in hers, *when nothing more could be done.* Her father *sat quite still . . . / especially not moving his eyes . . . / . . . motionless, alone, / with the dignity of a foreign leader.* He *kept silent to bear things.* The stillness is alive, the agar in which a microscopic fleck of his life takes hold in her. Hard to hold and hard to hope for, letting a loved one go, sitting with your own pain or next to another's, reaching for what comes from *things which are not.*

Neither of the pulls to focus narrowly or to see the big picture is a completed process. When the darkness turns to cede territory to contemplation of the next thing, I am a skeptic resisting conversion, reticent to see what is forming of the alchemy of sadness and loss, the reshaping of life in the context of ongoing grief and degeneration. I cannot yet see the new thing clearly; some days I do not even sense that it is out there. At times, the notion of a new thing seems some twisted tool that I am using to pry some good out of Ike's decline, to placate, to get through a day. How could there be waking, newness, amid days that for Ike have a rambling that is sometimes desperate, sometimes frenetically list-making, a Sisyphean weaving and unraveling?

I sit motionless on the train, eyes on the spot where I last saw the towers. I think of these poems that name places where nothing more can be done and where things are not. I think of those who lost so much on September 11, and with effort I push my mind further open to others who have lost. I cannot grasp that huge picture whole, only the caption beneath it—"All." I force my mind and heart to creak open. The words of Anne Reeve Aldrich's "Fraternity" enter. *I ask not how thy suffering came, / . . . To my large pity all's the same. / We will not speak of what we know, / Rehearse the pang, nor count the throe, / Let us draw close, and clasp the hand*, and whisper the password, *"I understand!"*

Losses are not retrievable. They are not setbacks. In the blankness left, perhaps other things come, a new thing, a different shape for the last thing's recollection.

Where the World Trade Center towers used to be, two blue pillars of light reached skyward last September 11. Now, more permanent fencing, repaved sidewalks, and improved pedestrian access frame the space. The feel of a demolition site is being displaced by the energy of a construction site.

I look for the *still depth* moving.

Shards

TEXT

It has taken me forty years to admit
emotions have no words.
I express and repress, scrawl
vowels on a placemat,

test my artistry
against a poor drawing of the Acropolis.
Find me wanting.
Which is not to say that as a man

I am inarticulate by nature, or that the sunshine
moves through the sugar shaker
and then through me without stopping.
Or that even as someone who learns

in metaphor, I am much different from
the sparrow outside the Greek diner,
atop the crusted snow,
brainless with hunger.

On my walk back from town this morning,
I met a woman in her driveway,
one hand on a snowblower. Weeping.
The enormous trumpet of the red machine

blew the powder into the air,
noise going nowhere as she wept.
They seemed to me as one,
she and her machine, and what could I do—

the placemat folded in my pocket
sang itself a pretty lie.
What could I say? Sorry.
Then she realized I had stopped:

she smiled badly, wiped her nose,
and went back to tidying.
And I went back to trudging through
words, head down, humming out of tune.

—ALAN MICHAEL PARKER

I am desperately sad. The news from the doctor hits hard. Subcortical dementia. For two days the research into those words keeps me busy. Now I have a notion, at least, of Ike's likely cognitive decline. Day three, an avalanche of sadness stuns me.

I am alone in the apartment, trying to work, and a single word comes, unsought and insistent, over and over—*shard*. I speak it out loud and listen to it. I wonder where it comes from, whether it is meant to bring relief and how it might. The sorrow feels impenetrable, even corrosive. I cannot get around it. It seems unfair to call a friend, to use another for my own comfort. Friends could offer an illusion or a feeling, but I am *atop the crusted snow, / brainless with hunger* for things to be other than they are. None of us can change things with Ike. No friend. No husband. No parent. No sibling. Nothing I can say or do. No bargaining position. The pain of it is unspeakable.

> *It has taken me forty years to admit*
> *emotions have no words.*

Utter pain.

> *. . . a snowblower. Weeping.*
> *The enormous trumpet of the red machine*

blew the powder into the air,
noise going nowhere as she wept.

The machine of my sadness is deafening and inescapable; it is all of me.

Shard. I go to the living room and turn the whisper-thin pages of the unabridged dictionary and consider the word's meanings. *Shard* shares an Anglo-Saxon root with *shear*. *Shard* suggests beauty in a way that *piece* and *fragment* do not. "The precious dish broke into shards of beauty on the board," *Webster's* offers.

I think of breaking open sun-bleached sand dollars to find doves. I remember art history class and a Grecian urn extrapolated from a few shards. Shards of pottery, of shells, suggest the whole. With this illness on this particular day, I do not glimpse a whole.

Find me wanting.
Which is not to say that as a man

I am inarticulate by nature, or that the sunshine
moves through the sugar shaker
and then through me without stopping.

I am mouth open, mute. My son's illness is refractory, bending and breaking apart things passed through it.

I look for, I need, words, lines, even ones falling short, maybe lying, incomplete, imperfect.

Shard and its form, *sherd*, I read, have two other meanings—first, a boundary, and second, a gap in a fence or wall. The word that means brokenness and beauty brings more— dividing lines and breaks in them, permeability in the seemingly impenetrable.

Words slip in. First, a shard, then more sought . . . *what could I do— / . . . What could I say?* The woman with the snowblower and the one with *the placemat folded in my pocket* continue, *tidying. / And . . . trudging through / words, head down, humming out of tune.* There *is* a text this morning.

Making Light

THE STARE'S NEST BY MY WINDOW

The bees build in the crevices
Of loosening masonry, and there
The mother birds bring grubs and flies.
My wall is loosening, honey-bees,
Come build in the empty house of the stare.

We are closed in, and the key is turned
On our uncertainty; somewhere
A man is killed, or a house burned,
Yet no clear fact to be discerned:
Come build in the empty house of the stare.

A barricade of stone or of wood;
Some fourteen days of civil war;
Last night they trundled down the road

That dead young soldier in his blood:
Come build in the empty house of the stare.

We had fed the heart on fantasies,
The heart's grown brutal from the fare;
More substance in our enmities
Than in our love; O honey-bees,
Come build in the empty house of the stare.

—W. B. YEATS

———

Last night, as I was sleeping
I dreamt—marvelous error!—
that I had a beehive
here inside my heart.
And the golden bees
were making white combs
and sweet honey
from my old failures.

—from "Last night, as I was sleeping"
by ANTONIO MACHADO
(translated by Robert Bly)

"*I*ke seems happy," Dr. Lynch said to me once Ike had left us to return to the waiting room.

"Yes," I replied. I did not want Dr. Lynch to consider me pessimistic, but these visits came only twice a year, and saying fully what I had been observing was important. I pushed myself to continue. "I think he is happy, in part, because he's lost some awareness."

"I'm glad you see that," Dr. Lynch said. "I agree."

He described subcortical dementia and gave context to Ike's tangential, out-there, winging-in-from-left-field, conversation-stopping comments. He gave me a "particular" understanding of an aspect of degeneration, freeing me from the imperial "general." From what he said, I saw that we would be less frustrated with Ike and he with himself if we now stayed as much as possible in the domains of emotion and memory and left aside conversations and activities that rely on reasoning and judgment.

With blood pounding in my ears following near disaster on the insane fast-lane merge ramp of I-76 along the Schuylkill River after we left the hospital, I recalled the words of the neuropsychologist from two winters earlier. Dr. Mark Brooks had evaluated Ike and first documented his cognitive decline. Ike had been raging and hurting from his college experience, his father and I from not having been able to foresee it or to protect him. Dr. Brooks had offered a forward-projected sort of consolation that a time would come when Ike would be less aware and it would be easier. I did not clearly comprehend all of what Dr. Brooks meant then, what "easier" would look like and for whom. For Ike? For us? Some of it I understood hypothetically, at arm's length, allowing no closer this horrible thing we were supposed to look forward to. Like wishing someone dead.

In early 2004 Ike's rage had subsided. I could see then that I had witnessed the two-year dying of a dream.

Dreams of my *own* have died swiftly and catastrophically at times. At others, their slipping away over decades has been barely perceptible, most painful awareness insulated with ample denial and distraction. Ike's dreams are falling away in chunks that echo the loss of gray and white matter. A loss, then a holding, a breather of sorts, then another loss, like a creek bank eroded from beneath by water moving close by.

During Ike's three weeks with us that December, we observed the change that Dr. Brooks had earlier suggested. Dr. Lynch had observed it, recorded it, and made it real in the way doctors do. Symptoms are fully born, it seems, when they are written into the clinical notes; such is the constitutive power of words.

I made for myself a simplified crib sheet on a mental three-by-five card—emotion and memory, yes; reason and judgment, no. The task in front of us after seeing Dr. Lynch was to buy Ike something to wear for basketball before taking him back to Soltane. The version of the game he plays

on Sundays at Soltane is modified, but his adulation of the
stars of the game—Allen Iverson, Vince Carter, Shaquille
O'Neal, Kevin Garnett—is as everyday regular as that of
the guys down the block. Ike wanted a superstar's jersey, but
he had no clue about where to go to buy one. Why had he
not asked someone at Soltane where the sporting goods
stores were that would have the type of jersey he wanted?
That would be the logical thing to do, right? My reasoning
mind, set to berate mode, tripped over itself. Wake up,
woman. Did you not hear the doctor? Skirt reasoning and
judgment; go for emotion. All Ike really needed was to get
something to wear for basketball and to feel good about the
process.

On the way into Target, helping Ike from the car, I
handed him his cane and turned my right shoulder to receive his left hand, the way we generally maneuvered when
we did not have his scooter—his cane in his right hand, his
left hand on my shoulder. Sometimes he did not want to
admit needing the shoulder.

"Hey, my shoulder needs you, Ike. It's lonely."

"What?" He laughed the full-body laugh that comes out
sometimes like a single explosion, sometimes like repeated
ammunition fire. This one was the single-explosion variety,
accompanied by a look of surprised delight. "What are you
talking about, Mom?"

"Well, look at it. Does my shoulder get used regularly
for anything very interesting? Really, carrying a pocket-

book, that's pretty boring." I checked to make sure he was catching the jest and saw the gorgeous smile that I know the girls notice when they look past his tremors and labored walk. "But when you're around, that shoulder has a whole reason for being. Here, make my shoulder happy, Ike."

He grinned and put his left hand there, and we made our slow, wobbly trek to the door. Emotion over reasoning. Good.

Inside the store, it was easier than I had anticipated to shift Ike from the search for a superstar jersey to a focus on the color choices. He has always had strong reactions to colors, a major feature of his descriptions when he was young.

"Hey, look at these, Ike." On one rack were shorts, jerseys, warm-up pants, and long-sleeved zip-up jackets, entire ensembles in four combinations—red, blue, green, and black/silver. The black/silver, reversible, caught Ike's eye, and I searched for his size. The NBA greats flew out the door.

I went with Ike into the men's dressing room. Two years earlier, even six months earlier, this would have embarrassed both of us. Now I knew it was the only way to get the job done. The dressing-room attendant looked up as we passed. My determined look kept her quiet. She read in it, Don't even ask; I know what I'm doing. When had I come to know? This was not premeditated. And it was a first.

In the dressing room, I wanted to be efficient and quick and minimize any embarrassment Ike might begin to feel.

He moves very slowly. He has trouble lifting his legs. When he is sitting, he has come to rely on lifting them by pulling up with his hands clasped beneath his thighs. I knelt to lift each foot in and out of the pants. I organized tops and bottoms, showing him the different options, and I tried to keep him positive and upbeat and happy and moving, the mood light, checking the fit. These were my jobs in the tight little dressing room with my grown son. Between outfits, I called my sister-in-law on my cell phone to let her know that our very important basketball attire acquisition mission would prevent our stopping by to visit. Ike and I had a good time, and he liked his purchase. He put his hand on my shoulder on the way out without my coaxing. He seemed to feel triumphant, and so did I. It had been made better by making light.

Hard truths are hard to tell and to hear. I think of Dr. Lynch's efforts that January to help me get a handle on Ike's mental capacities and Dr. Brooks's prediction two years earlier and its intention to encourage. I think also of Dr. Goldstein in the year in between, pulling up Ike's MRI scans on his computer screen and comparing them with a "normal" brain scan so that I could actually see the atrophy, the smoothing, the loss of crucial convolutions. Dr. Marc Patterson, who had examined Ike in 2001, reminded me recently that the word *doctor* at its root means "teacher." Any of these doctors could have done less. It might have been easier to have done less. Enrolled in a course not of my choosing, with doctors teaching lessons that perhaps they would rather not, I was being offered learning I truly needed.

The word *patient* at its root means "sufferer," one who endures suffering. *Passion* comes from the Latin verb *patire*, "to suffer." Patient connotes a posture of waiting, passion a force of emotion anything but passive. Patient passion and passionate patience pull at conceptual seams. Poems sometimes inhabit this dialectic. Seamus Heaney says in his 1995 Nobel lecture that the best in poetry is "tender minded towards life itself . . . and tough-minded about what happens in and to life." Heaney speaks specifically about the Yeats poem "The Stare's Nest by My Window."

> It knows that the massacre will happen again on the roadside, that the workers in the minibus are going to be lined up and shot down just after quitting time; but it also credits as a reality the squeeze of the hand, the actuality of sympathy and protectiveness between living creatures. It satisfies the contradictory needs which consciousness experiences at times of extreme crisis, the need on the one hand for a truth telling that will be hard and retributive, and on the other hand, the need not to harden the mind to a point where it denies its own yearnings for sweetness and trust.

Palimpsest. There is no virgin building ground. The bees make their home where masonry is loosening, where starlings have moved on from their feedings of grubs and flies. *Come build.* It is odd, ludicrous in fact, to imagine a patient and doctor in our situation saying that to one another. What could be built here in this life of my son's? In mine with him? In these relationships with the people caring for him and teaching us about him?

Build, in the midst of crumbling—*loosening masonry . . . / My wall is loosening?* In the midst of ambiguity—*the key is turned / On our uncertainty; somewhere / . . . no clear fact to be discerned?* In the midst of tragedy—*That dead young soldier in his blood?* In the midst of previous failed attempts to come to terms—*We had fed the heart on fantasies?* In the midst of the consequences of those earlier failures—*The heart's grown brutal from the fare?* Build here amid sadness, decline, loss, dashed dreams, and reams of information about disorders and protein and fat chains and cellular metabolism? Here? Yeats's poem says that other things have been at work all along.

In the first and last verse, the honeybees are invited to come build in the empty house of the stare. Starlings collect in loud, noisy flocks and, with their iridescent blackish plumage and long bill, yellow in spring and summer, are generally considered a nuisance, an enemy to smaller, more desirable birds. They mimic other birds' songs and other sounds, and they build nests usually in houses and outbuildings. In the poem, they have deserted. Bees are an altogether different sort—quietly, diligently moving in choreographed harmony. *The bees build in the crevices / Of loosening masonry,* in the cracks of a place more full of enmity than love.

Machado places the bees *inside my heart* where *old failures* are spun into combs and sweet, redeeming honey.

I want the doctors, the teachers, to know the words of Heaney and Yeats and Machado, to know how vital are words often easier left unsaid, how the hard truth can be something you stand on to see a little light.

In the Details

THE DISENFRANCHISED, GRIEVING

quote not able to grieve unquote

from this view nothing melts
all available surfaces coalesce into one
and then there are those outside the surface

children
or the developmentally disabled
or women

outside the running together of time
and the person missing in such a way
as to bring about an equation that is not equal

> *infertility or miscarriage*
> *or abortion or*

there being not quite here
I return to absence
this not quite

> *or pet or an ex-spouse*

inside the mind there is loss
which resembles distance
but is grief at work

> *in time there is a lessening*

the way
I bled and bled
without living

—LYNN KILPATRICK

*I*n a favorite photograph, Ike, a proud, chubby two-year-old, sits squarely on our old thrift-store couch, the white, grippy bottoms of his slippers squared up at the lower edge of the frame. His hair and deep blue eyes shine, the irregular hairline across his forehead brings back home haircuts in the upstairs bathroom. His expression, head cocked to the side, chin up, is all pride and joy. A blue terry-cloth robe wraps around his shoulders. Beneath it, across his chest, an orange-gold T-shirt peeks out. Even then, he liked sleeping in soft T-shirts.

Across Ike's lap is the source of his barely contained jubilation. Propped on two throw pillows, their black cotton covers embroidered with multicolored birds, is his brother. It is his first day home from the hospital. Nick, days old, appears to have been plopped there, his head, over which he had no control, settled chin down into his chest, his two tiny arms stick-straight, one gripping the pillow cover, the other midair in front of his brother. Ike has one arm between the pillows and Nick's head. His other hand, square and block-like, rests on his brother's abdomen. Obviously the arrangement has been staged, the boys posed by adults, yet their expressions of complete comfort and mutual connection are readily apparent.

So much is in the details, so much depends on pulling into relief figures often overlooked in the indistinct ground of taken-for-granted. Especially in grieving, particular details, seemingly small items, can trigger a flood of awareness of things lost. In the allegorical tale of Anodos in *Phantastes*, George MacDonald writes, "The merest trifles sometimes rivet the attention in deepest misery." Yesterday it was a pottery bowl at the back of a high shelf rarely reached—a reminder of the hopes Ike had held in high school when he had carefully fashioned it, smooth and symmetrical. I felt ambushed, as if the small green vessel had been lying in wait.

I have an accordion file of mementos that, although not collected with that intent, has become a catalog of things Ike can no longer do. In first grade on family trips he would busy himself practicing his D'Nealian script in a little yellow notebook, one sentence on a page. With the precisely curling tails that would make the transition to cursive easy—according to his teacher, Mrs. Mitchell—one short sentence reads, "Daddy, I can run!"

A program from the end-of-middle-school ceremony in eighth grade, when Ike had been chosen by his classmates as one of two speakers and he had walked to the stage and mounted the podium and spoken from the text he had written himself. Not a hint of a limp, then, and no straying, confused mind. A program from his high school graduation, where he had walked with great difficulty—uncles, grandparents, all whispering wishes that he not fall—where a classmate who had a crush on him for a few weeks in ninth grade before he was labeled "weird" extended him an arm to balance as they descended the few steps from the stage. That graduation ceremony consisted of the words, music, and performances of the seniors. Ike, ten days back from his first trek to Mayo Clinic, had contributed his presence.

Swimming goggles. Swimming, a strength of Ike's in eighth grade and in the first years of his illness in ninth and tenth grades, then became less about his legs and more about his shoulders and chest hauling his lower half through the water. Going to the pool became more about scraped feet bleeding when dragged on concrete surfaces.

There are the papers that he wrote in ninth and tenth grades and the evidence of decline in eleventh and twelfth and the ten weeks of college—hard to discern then, painfully apparent now. Some of these I have not been able to keep, as if throwing them away would erase Ike's decline. I put the school papers back and pick up again the little yellow book with Ike's proud first-grade proclamation, no longer true, his handwriting then neater and smaller than now. I imagine inhaling that shred of time sixteen years ago when Ike was bright beginnings and hopeful eagerness. I imagine others who have lost and are trying to fill in and hold on to clear, tangible details. So much of living and so much of grieving, so much of knowing what is there and what has gone depends on the details.

Ike's letters home from summer camp in middle school were studied and conscientious and kind, the height of his ability to communicate in words. His notes now are to-do lists, memory aids, stilted and sometimes awkward, signed "your firstborn son" and then a monogram-type signature worked and reworked. From murky awareness, he is reaching for forms, symbols, and surfaces, clear edges, sharply defined details. Of course, to his family, his communications are still precious even as they are painful. To others, they must seem odd, sometimes incomprehensible, perhaps annoying. Several times in recent years I have explained

Ike's illness to old friends who were confused about what he was trying to say in letters or e-mails or phone calls. We are learning together to view Ike's communications as finite snippets of connection taken at face value, uncoupled from usual expectations of follow-up. Simply making contact often seems to satisfy Ike now.

These details of Ike's life color in and flesh out the MRIs' black-and-white snapshots of atrophy. He is living through a slippage, but he is living, as are we who love him. It has felt at times as if I have been suspended, nowhere in particular, for eight years, deferred, held in abeyance, on hold—*the way / I bled and bled / without living*. Seeing the distinct details of the embedded grief suggests instead the alternative of giving power to or enfranchising grieving, taking it on fully, unabashedly.

Measures and indicators suggest manageability. The simple desire to measure validates. We do not usually take stock of things we regard as insignificant. In the first four years of Ike's illness I kept a detailed listing of his symptoms and the time frames of major changes, in part because the medical records I toted to specialists needed narration. I have recorded his cognitive and physical decline since that time in a less-organized way, but the changes are there in e-mails and journals and on calendars.

Focusing on details may be in part an attempt to halt the dynamic, but it is also for me a mindful noticing, a way to avoid the place where, in Lynn Kilpatrick's lines, *nothing melts* and *all available surfaces coalesce into one*. It is a way to inhabit a place inside the *running together of time*, inside *the surface*, an effort to balance the equation. I would rather ask when suffering will end or when it will no longer ambush me; yet asking when it will change shape, when my experience of it will be different and how—these questions create a perspective that, while not hospitable, is habitable.

When a telephone conversation becomes one in which Ike gets stuck on "you know I mean you know I mean" so many times that he loses what he was trying to say and falls silent, when I look through the window of the restaurant at 77th and Amsterdam at a "normal" family having dinner together and know that what it looks like from the outside will never again be mine, when I see and feel in sharp detail for a minute or two, this is life precise and it is mine. It is very much here; there is not a *not quite* about it. I know that on the other end of the telephone line is a young man who will hang up the phone and laugh at something someone at Soltane says and move on as best he can.

Details can be chosen, edited. I can claim a different restaurant scene, one with a good view of the spot on the sidewalk where Ike parks his scooter. Accommodating simply, they give us the table next to the window. Nick is there too, and we eat Southwest and everyone tries something new. I warn Nick, "Be careful. Don't get Ike laughing. He's just put guacamole in his mouth." There is probably no one inside or passing by who would consider us "normal," but we are living with the loss and the lessening—inside, *grief at work*, living.

I can hold details and know they are there, let go and know they once were. The way my grandmother's Buick smelled of clove chewing gum, the Richie Rich funny books she bought us in Southern Pines—my missing her takes some of its shape from the shape she occupied when she was here. I start a list of the things that Ike enjoys—a way to see the present moment as specifically as I have been chronicling the decline. Today, I make plans to take him to a basketball game at his brother's college. I send him dried apricots for Valentine's Day.

Central Park Boathouse

———————

This is the bright home
in which I live,
this is where
I ask
my friends
to come,
this is where I want
to love all the things
it has taken me so long
to learn to love.

This is the temple
of my adult aloneness
and I belong
to that aloneness
as I belong to my life.

There is no house
like the house of belonging.

> —from "The House of Belonging"
> by DAVID WHYTE

I thought we would love New York. What I did not know was how New York would infuse itself into me, refusing to let me hide out. At least I did not know it with the intensity I was to experience.

There were choices. New York was not forced on us. Ike is at Camphill Soltane outside of Philadelphia; Noah's mom in New Jersey. Noah's work could be shifted back to New Jersey, and my writing was portable. We looked for the city to enliven us, give us the energy to pick up our marriage again or the space to put it down. As we apartment hunted, I watched Noah's shoulders un-hunch a bit, his expression lighten, his step quicken.

Maybe at midlife, with the nest newly empty, belonging would have a new feel, and perhaps with Ike's degenerative illness, a sense of exile or apartness would color it. *This is the temple / of my adult aloneness / and I belong / to that aloneness / as I belong to my life.*

> *. . . In the meantime*
> *There are bills to be paid, machines to keep in repair,*

Irregular verbs to learn, the Time Being to redeem
From insignificance. The happy morning is over,
The night of agony still to come; the time is noon:
When the Spirit must practice his scales of rejoicing
Without even a hostile audience, and the Soul endure
A silence that is neither for nor against her faith

—from *For the Time Being*
by W. H. AUDEN

In my first days in the city, alone in a hotel near the apartment, awaiting the moving van, two routines—getting up early to write and leaving my writing midafternoon to run—framed my days. Inside that frame the city came to me. *In the meantime . . . the Time Being to redeem / From insignificance.* It was June, and I was a block from Central Park. Early one morning on my way for coffee I saw a father helping load his daughter's motorized wheelchair into his van. He appeared to be about my age, his daughter about Ike's, and her physical disabilities looked severe. He was maneuvering his daughter and her equipment unremarkably, and that to me seemed remarkable.

On my walks at either end of my runs in Central Park, I passed elderly people in wheelchairs, parked with their caretakers. Some of the people appeared lively and engaged, some did not, yet there they were every day, getting their piece of sunshine and outdoor time. *The Spirit must practice his scales of rejoicing.* How public and shared life in a city is;

"out there" with disability or age, comeliness or homeliness, it is all so matter-of-fact. Living in Atlanta, our sadness was as big as we were, and it traveled with us everywhere we went. Always in cars, I did not have the opportunity to see in passing people whose suffering might resemble ours. We were not walking or pushing a wheelchair or riding a motorized scooter four blocks to the grocery store or across the park to the museum. In Atlanta, while usually supportively watched, we were watched, and we were an anomaly. A measure of our coping was taken by even the most well-meaning.

Maybe part of the salve of New York is simply the size. When there are millions of us, there are going to be more with afflictions, pains that might look like mine. Joys that might look like mine too. The truism "everybody's got something" seems all the truer with so many right in front of you, within reach, every day.

It was two days before Christmas, an unusually warm and dry day for that time of year. Nick and Noah would be joining us that night, but for the day, it was just Ike and me. Like old times, when he, my firstborn, was my main daytime companion. So close back then, I could read Ike's moods, feel his thoughts almost before they formed. He had been a chubby toddler in Oshkosh overalls, everything about him solid. And he was happy for hours at a stretch in the large garden at our first home and during long days at the univer-

sity day care when I went back to work. Not a trouble-
maker, it seemed then he did not have to push hard against
life to secure his spot.

Getting out of the apartment sometime during the day
with Ike is important. This was true in August when he was
with me in Manhattan, and it continued to be true in the
three-week winter holiday from Soltane. In December, a bit
chilly for park benches, we sought indoor venues. I had
some writing to work on. Ike likes to read detective stories.
He has trouble telling you about them, but he loves to read
them, especially one particular series. Late morning, with
my writing and his book in the front basket of his scooter,
we headed for Central Park. I knew the boathouse grill had
space inside for his scooter.

As with the father putting his handicapped daughter into
the van the previous June, what was grand about this December day was its ordinariness. Ike and I could be together
out in the world in spite of his handicaps, and we could be
more than his handicaps. We could belong in the house of
a city too broad to be defined by his illness. None of the
passersby would know the "before" Ike. Many had "seen it
all," an "all" I could imagine more piercing than ours.
There was a salve of acceptance on this December 23,
something edging toward a sweet normalcy. We ordered
sandwiches and found a table where we could see the water
and park the scooter out of the way. There was little that
day that would from the outside seem significant, but it was,
for me, a precious *Time Being* redeemed.

Here, *where I want / to love all the things / it has taken me so long / to learn to love,* our world was peopled with tourists in the dressier dining room below, with its tablecloths and waiters; with regulars greeting one another by the fireplace, one or two of whom it was easy to imagine were park residents; with a British tourist poring over the books he took out of his Whitney Museum bag; with two men, obviously friends, who thought baseball was the best thing to talk about, even in December. We stayed for almost two hours. Near the end of the time, I read Ike a little of the story I had been revising. He offered comments, said I needed to tell more about the old man's children.

He's not chubby anymore, and some of his body's solidity now is rigidity, spasticity. But I love being with him out in the world in this city in much the same way that I enjoyed our days in our vegetable garden when he was small. On the way back to the apartment, I think, Maybe what people see when they see us, before or after Ike's impairment, is that we enjoy being together. Savoring the pleasure in this time is what I will hold. Quotidian, mundane, ordinary possibilities.

Slanted

———

ON PRAYER

You ask me how to pray to someone who is not.
All I know is that prayer constructs a velvet bridge
And walking it we are aloft, as on a springboard,
Above landscapes the color of ripe gold
Transformed by a magic stopping of the sun.
That bridge leads to the shore of Reversal
Where everything is just the opposite and the word is
Unveils a meaning we hardly envisioned.
Notice: I say we; *there, every one, separately,*
Feels compassion for others tangled in the flesh
And knows that if there is no other shore
We will walk that aerial bridge all the same.

—CZESLAW MILOSZ
(translated by Robert Hass)

A NOISELESS PATIENT SPIDER

A noiseless, patient spider,
I mark'd where on a little promontory it stood
  isolated,
Mark'd how to explore the vacant vast surrounding,
It launch'd forth filament, filament, filament, out of
  itself,
Ever unreeling them, ever tirelessly speeding them.

And you O my Soul where you stand,
Surrounded, surrounded, in measureless oceans of
  space,
Ceaselessly musing, venturing, throwing, seeking the
  spheres, to connect them,
Till the bridge you will need be form'd, till the
  ductile anchor hold,
Till the gossamer thread you fling, catch somewhere,
  O my Soul.

—WALT WHITMAN,
Leaves of Grass, #208

I grew up in the church. I had avoided thinking about miracles or assumed they were symbolic, not literal. Certainly, as a child, I had wished I could believe in them. As an adult, I have considered them nice ideas, a way to say that something wonderful has happened or an effort to put into words the beauty and awe of nature or childbirth, but not an actual counter-rational event. When Ike's illness appeared, I hoped for a turnaround or a slowdown, certainly, but it seemed silly and presumptuous to petition for a total healing. I had known plenty of sick people, and I knew personally of no miracles that looked like that. If I were forced to use the word *miracle*, I would work it and mold it into a shape more like the miracle of a new perspective. Most times, honestly, I avoided the word.

At different stages of the illness, I have avoided even the idea of God. Both of our sons did better than I with this. Both of them kept up their activities at church and pursued their understanding of the sadness of Ike's illness within the context of their taught religious beliefs more enthusiastically than I. Some of my strongest support at times was at church, from a generously broad-minded group who tolerated, even encouraged, dissonance and questioning. I did not have to leave completely in order to do battle. My faith, such as it was, was shaky. Some brave people face profound suffering and grief and never waver. I was not one of them.

Bruce Springsteen's "Countin' on a Miracle," from his post–9/11 CD, says "We've got no fairytale ending." I could buy that. The next line says "In God's hands our fate is complete." He arrived at that quickly; I paused.

When I entertained the concept of God, it would take the form of a dare or a challenge. Why not show me you are there? What is the point in a God who obscures or hides out? How is that loving? For long stretches of time, I could hear no answer.

Then a verse, heard one Sunday, suggested Jesus confessing his own perplexity: "The wind blows where it wills, and you hear the sound of it, but you do not know whence it comes or whither it goes; so it is with . . . the Spirit." (John 3:8) Less an explanation to me than an encouragement, I took heart that among the "insiders," within the Trinity, was acknowledgment of mystery. Mystery was more approachable than miracle. Contemplation would do. Wondering about meaning could be prayer. Things did not have to be seen straight on in order to be seen.

Czeslaw Milosz's poem reminds me of the humanity of asking for a God. Even *if there is no other shore / We will walk that aerial bridge all the same.* The poem emphasizes the plural: *I say we; there, every one, separately.* Constructing the velvet bridge and walking it aloft *as on a springboard*, feeling compassion, scarcely grasping meaning—these are things *we* do, not me in isolation. In the poem, humanity seeks divinity, *the shore of Reversal / Where everything is just the opposite . . .* The way there is up and over, into ripe, transformed terrain; what is found there is a new way of being, where . . . is / *Unveils a meaning we hardly envisioned*. The poem has a tentative feel that is not too foreign to imagine from my position of doubt, when it did not seem time for "A Mighty Fortress Is Our God" or "All Glory, Laud and Honor."

Yet, at times, I drift away from this poem as well. When a new dose of deterioration is evident and the pain resurges, mystery can be annoying, and I am again irritated with a God who would choose veiling and hiding out. I have heard many personal stories of faith in my years in the church, many ways in which people have indicated that they saw God working out a purpose in their lives. Just recently a friend in his fifties told me about his fall out of the sixth-floor window of an apartment building when he was eighteen months old. "I wasn't even hurt. Looking back, I think, Guess it's clear whose hands I was in." I love hearing this story—an individual sharing his personal truth-making machinery—yet it also perplexes me. If the reasoning is played in reverse, what do I do with the outwardly *not* blessed? Does it follow from my friend's story that since Ike *is* hurt, that we know in whose hands he is *not*?

I have often needed different slants. I keep casting about. Walt Whitman's poem puts words to what has felt like the consistent inconsistency of my faith—*Ceaselessly musing, venturing, throwing—seeking the spheres, to connect them*. Poetry does partiality well. A part can suggest a larger whole or be all in itself. A parabola and a parable, the meaning may be in the coming close, in the approach. I am not a pillar of strength. I am riddled with weaknesses and incompleteness, tentative and uncertain enough for Milosz's velvet bridge and Whitman's anchor of gossamer thread precisely to suffice. Ike's illness is only grasped in part; perhaps God is too; and maybe also in that partiality is loving.

Some painters and photographers use intentionally incomplete points of view, raking angles, severely cropped images, avoidance of a grounding horizon line to destabilize the observer, to coax involvement by making the viewer's perspective a conscious feature of the work. A theater stage can use a "rake," a different inclination or slope, an angle to alter the audience's perspective. A different "slant" on things brings Ike's slanted walk to mind. Is it an angle from which I can glimpse God?

Along with a Life

---

the one central spot of red
—the wonderful thing which,
whether in a fairy story or a word or a human being,
is the life and depth—
whether of truth or humour or pathos—
the eye to the face of it—
the thing that shows the unknowable

—from "Imagination"
by GEORGE MACDONALD

From a secondhand book vendor on Columbus Avenue on a cold February Saturday, William Carlos Williams's book *The Embodiment of Knowledge* leaped out at me; I bought it. In the introduction to the volume, Ron Loewinsohn puts Williams in the company of those who did not see knowledge as power, knowledge as a tool for the pursuit of inhuman perfection, or knowledge as transcendence of physical things. According to Loewinsohn, Williams was

> a member of that sanest line of development in our history, those thinkers and artists who insist on the *integrity* of the human organism—thought *and* feeling, sense *and* intellection, mind *and* body . . . [He] takes his place in a line of development that goes back at least as far as Herakleitos, who also knew that "To take thought thickens the blood around the heart." (pp. xxiv, xxv)

A poet and a doctor, and his thoughts on knowing—I devoured the book before dinner. It is a collection of essays for his two sons, found among his papers at Yale's Beinecke Library and published posthumously. Williams instructed that it be "printed as it is, faults and all," and he dedicated it "To My Boys . . . intended to go along *with a life* [emphasis his] and to be in no sense its objective." The choice of words in his dedication is telling. Williams saw knowledge as something to go along with a life, not as life's purpose. Knowledge and ignorance for Williams were partial processes. He writes:

> Knowledge is essential, delightful, human . . . the codified sum of knowledge is stupid and inhuman—unless we

achieve toward it the same relationship that we find most essential, delightful, human in any of its parts. Unless we stand beyond it and not it beyond us to order us . . .

What kind of a mind . . . is most likely to make useful discoveries . . . [T]he mind which will be humane in its perceptions and skilled in transverse, not perpendicular ways. The earth is round.

—from *Embodiment of Knowledge*, pp. 63–64

Not knowing has felt at times like torment. At various points Ike has raged at the unknown thing that is undoing him. Suffering an illness of unknown cause is a devaluing nonstatus, relegating to perpetual exile, habeas corpus indefinitely suspended. In it, an individual must create his own status.

On the other hand, labels can pigeonhole and lop off a story before its intended ending. Cancer patients can read too much into their disease's stage classification and forget that stories emerge from the margins and defy a label's implications. A physician spoke recently about the dangers of a noninformative diagnosis, one that carries no prescriptive measures and the threat of pigeonholing rather than care. Many people have experienced the negative aspects of a diagnosis, "writing them off" when nothing can be done. All virtue is not in deduction.

Knowledge is not a field beyond a fence that we hop

over. The boundaries between the known and the unknown become more flexible and movable, more analogous to Japanese screens. Knowing is an interplay between itself and ignorance, itself and what it is not. So too might be the comprehension of an illness. As surely as I think I have it cornered—knowledge or wisdom or insight—fenced in, partitioned off, it defies me, that *one central spot of red . . . the eye to the face of it— / the thing that shows the unknowable.* Flexibility can stave off despair. Even temporarily, absence of knowledge need not be absence of meaning.

Houses and Hearts

THE HOUSE ON THE HILL

They are all gone away
The House is shut and still,
There is nothing more to say.

Through broken walls and gray
The winds blow bleak and shrill:
They are all gone away.

Nor is there one to-day
To speak them good or ill:
There is nothing more to say.

Why is it then we stray
Around the sunken sill?
They are all gone away.

And our poor fancy-play
For them is wasted skill:
There is nothing more to say.

There is ruin and decay
In the House on the Hill:
They are all gone away,
There is nothing more to say.

—EDWIN ARLINGTON ROBINSON

When sharp sadness spills out, I wonder where the energy goes, whether it reverberates or joins other wailings, spending itself or multiplying in unseen places. It seems too powerful to do nothing or go nowhere. I worry that mine might bother others.

Many times I hold the sadness in; many times this seems better. No one would want to visit this sad house where sad work needs to be done. Even when I go to the meetings and the games and the parties and the dinners, I am in this house, Robinson's "House on the Hill." Kind friends wait *around the sunken sill*, but they sense and I know that *There is nothing more to say*. Words, at other times comforting, fall short. When Edward R. Murrow ended his report on what he had just seen at Buchenwald, he said, "For most of it I have no words."

Houses permeate our human ordering of the world—our thinking and living and playing, often our dreams. I played house as a child with my cousins on weekend and summer afternoons in the "reeds," a stand of bamboo in my grandmother's yard. Many of the details of that play have faded, but images of structure and roles flow back, how the places where the reeds were more openly spaced were living rooms, the smaller places bedrooms and closets, and how the more assertive among us were parents, initiators of actions, rulers of the domain, to which the rest of us responded. On the hill next to our home in the early sixties, my older brother played "fort." A friend had a vinyl-cloth "house" that fit over her mom's card table. We played in it for hours. There was Barbie's Dream House. When Trolls were the rage, we had shoebox houses with handkerchief sheets and cotton ball pillows. "Housing" occupied a lot of my childhood play.

In our sadness over Ike, Noah and I would occasionally stop and count the months that had passed in which we had invited no one into our home. It seemed that all we had to offer in our house was not anything anyone in their right mind would wish to share. Our house needed to be left alone, left still. We were not sure we wanted to occupy it.

BEREFT

Where had I heard this wind before
Change like this to a deeper roar?

What would it take my standing there for,
Holding open a restive door,
Looking down hill to a frothy shore?
Summer was past and day was past.
Somber clouds in the west were massed.
Out in the porch's sagging floor,
Leaves got up in a coil and hissed,
Blindly struck at my knee and missed.
Something sinister in the tone
Told me my secret must be known:
Word I was in the house alone
Somehow must have gotten abroad,
Word I was in my life alone,
Word I had no one left but God.

—ROBERT FROST

In Frost's "Bereft," the perspective is from inside the house looking out. The speaker holds open a door and looks out on *a frothy shore*, little of substance to hold his attention, aware of roaring and blind hissing and things somber, sagging, and sinister. *Word* has gotten out that he is alone but for God. The two words, *but God*—is that hope or resignation?

When nothing could be said to make Ike's situation any better, and when avoiding the focus on it has felt false, I have pulled away from friends and family. This has had its costs. I have missed years of closeness and sharing and the things that have gone on in others' lives. I miss knowing whether my godson likes school or lacrosse better, whether one friend has found something yet that really lights her up, how another is doing with her new job, another with his old. I am not justifying my pulling away, but trying to describe it and perhaps understand it. Maybe it is common among people caring for sick friends and family to miss great swatches of life with others and perhaps only to see it once the sick loved one has died. Maybe this loss of human connections is another face of the loss that illness is.

And maybe my isolation spares others. An intelligent friend recently described a corkscrew ratcheting down and down, round and round, plunging itself into the meat of the cork, implying that such was my process of "working" in isolation what is happening in my life with Ike. He was suggesting that this might not be for my own good. It made me consider how careful I need to be to watch out for friends, to make sure they do not get caught like fragile fingers in the grinding gears of this grief.

Maybe the reconnections will come, not in great shifts or stages that arrive and stay, but in little discrete packets in my life. Eudora Welty in *One Time, One Place* speaks about a parting of the curtain of indifference that veils one person from another. I imagine the curtain as pain, and I see it not being parted so much as fluttering open from time to time, as if at an open window by the shore. When the agony is heavy, the curtain hangs still; all of the energies are required within, at home. Explaining sufficiently to connect requires energy that is not always available. Often one of the most exhausting parts about trips to out-of-town specialists with Ike has been the reporting afterward to colleagues at work and our friends and family, the obligation to keep others informed.

Some relationships become reduced to two-way reporting sessions. Others go away entirely for a while. Some become communicate-in-December-only friendships. In some, we have moved out of each other's lives; in some, we are in a holding pattern, circling, waiting to land someday.

DEVOTION

The heart can think of no devotion
Greater than being shore to the ocean—
Holding the curve of one position,
Counting an endless repetition.

—ROBERT FROST

It is a goal, at least, to hold steady, to be the shore to the other's ocean.

As sappy and overexposed as hearts are as symbols of love, I treasure a few made for me as gifts. One is a green, crinkly paper heart with a blue pocket and a pearly button stitched on. Inside the pocket my friend placed a verse and an illustration, both her own creations. The verse is about vulnerability and breathing and dreaming. This friend is much of what I am not. She lives her life on the outside—exuberant and hospitable. I imagine grief for her would look like a big banquet table with people crowded around, engaged in multiple simultaneous conversations, her grieving readily on the outside with no need to sequester herself. I appreciate her. I thank her for giving me a heart and something of her in it, for being at the shore and holding the curve and continuing to be who she is.

THE HUMAN HEART

We construct it from tin and ambergris and clay,
       ochre, graph paper, a funnel
        of ghosts, whirlpool
in a downspout full of midsummer rain.

It is, for all its freedom and obstinance,
       an artifact of human agency
        in its maverick intricacy,
its chaos reflected in earthly circumstance,

its appetites mirrored by a hungry world
       like the lights of the casino
        in the coyote's eye. Old
as the odor of almonds in the hills around Solano,

filigreed and chancelled with flavor of blood oranges,
fashioned from moonlight,
yarn, nacre, cordite,
shaped and assembled valve by valve, flange by flange,

and finished with the carnal fire of interstellar dust.
We build the human heart
and lock it in its chest
and hope that what we have made can save us.

—CAMPBELL MCGRATH

In four sentences, two longer ones between a shorter one and a fragment, the poem says of the heart—that we make it, of what we make it, and what we do with it and why. McGrath's poem reimages the heart in tangible, even earthy detail, *tin, clay, ochre,* but there are also *ghosts, moonlight,* and *interstellar dust.* There is a *coyote* and evidence of other animals—*ambergris, nacre.* In these and in *whirlpool, downspout, rain,* there is water. As if with synesthesia, I smell a taste, *the odor of almonds,* and taste a vision, *filigreed and chancelled with flavor.* Enigmatic, the heart demands more than a unitary experience. Both *artifact,* a human construction, and *maverick,* a renegade, it knows chaos and hunger, beauty and explosiveness, yet it is also ordered . . . *assembled valve by valve, flange by flange.* A thing unto itself and yet not, it reflects and mirrors, navigating the individual and the universal, the external and the internal.

The poem's lines end in soft and hard sounds. From the first stanza—with its *l* and *n* of *funnel, whirlpool,* and *rain*—to the second, softness dominates: *ce, cy* in *obstinance, agency, intricacy, circumstance.* In the fourth, *oranges, flange* wrap the harder-ending sounds of *moonlight, cordite.* In the final stanza, locking the heart away, three harder endings, *dust, heart, chest,* open in the last line to the softer *us.* The soft ending sounds cushion the heart's harsh ingredients.

Line lengths vary. Commas create a list of the surprising components. Then, with no punctuation, the line races on. I love the sounds in . . . *Old / as the odor of almonds in the hills around Solano.* Hearts, troublesome and troubling, are the context of human existence, its limitations and its hopes for transcending them.

By the poem's end, something dangerous has been made and locked away, fraught with the potential to destroy and to save. Should it be locked up, a prisoner, or a keepsake in a hope chest, or should it be put into play? Do I dare, since, after all, I know what it's made of?

MY HEART

I'm not going to cry all the time
nor shall I laugh all the time,
I don't prefer one "strain" to another.
I'd have the immediacy of a bad movie,
not just a sleeper, but also the big,
overproduced first-run kind. I want to be

at least as alive as the vulgar. And if
some aficionado of my mess says "That's
not like Frank!", all to the good! I
don't wear brown and grey suits all the time,
do I? No. I wear workshirts to the opera,
often. I want my feet to be bare,
I want my face to be shaven, and my heart—
you can't plan on the heart, but
the better part of it, my poetry, is open.

—FRANK O'HARA

Friends know that the condition of the house and the heart sometimes precludes openings. But not always. My cry will echo until my heart's pocket, *the better part of it*, opens to more.

Naming

_____

We learned the Whole of Love—
The Alphabet—the Words—
A Chapter—then the mighty Book—
Then—Revelation closed—

But in Each Other's eyes
An Ignorance beheld—
Diviner than the Childhood's—
And each to each, a Child—

Attempted to expound
What Neither—understood—
Alas, that Wisdom is so large—
And Truth—so manifold!

—EMILY DICKINSON, #568

W e decided on the name Isaac in June before his birth in December. It was an easy choice; its meaning, "he who laughs," held our first hope—that he be happy. When he reached high school, he added Ike, and I found I LIKE IKE and I LIKE IKE EVEN BETTER campaign buttons from the fifties at a flea market. Ike did not replace Isaac; he is called both interchangeably, almost equally.

Name has numerous roots coming from a range of Indo-European languages. Naming is an important way toward making sense of things, ordering the world and interacting with it. Names are appellations, there for the purpose of calling. The Latin root is akin to *noscere*, *gnoscere*, "to know," the same root for diagnosis, knowing, or discerning one thing from another.

The origins of the word *laugh* are presumed mimetic, naming it what it sounded like, the guttural reflex—laugh. *Webster's* defines *laughter* as an expression of mirth peculiar to the human species. A quick list of its synonyms—*giggles*, *chortles*, *chuckles*, *hoots*, *cackles*, *sniggers*, and *guffaws*—evokes it. Some scholars suggest that laughter's biologic origins were a shared response to passing danger and the residue of trust among those who had jointly survived a close-call experience. Laughing and trusting are both in the roots of Isaac's name.

A neurologist recently suggested that given the current

directions in genetic research and genome mapping, it is likely that what is affecting Ike has more than one locus of responsibility. Many disorders are being attributed to multiple gene locales, interactions, and cross-reactions. After these years of hoping for a disease name, we may end up with more than one.

Identity has multiple sources, myriad ways to claim it, and a galvanizing core. Complexity and multiplicity can be as reassuring and freeing as simplicity and unity. *Wisdom is so large— / And Truth—so manifold!*

A cylindrical pipe fitting with multiple lateral outlets, carbon copies, the multiple stomachs of ruminant animals—manifold are names and truths. In Emily Dickinson's poem, the serious effort of studying the entirety leads to the humbling of divine ignorance in a crucible in which the most ardent attempts to understand are ground down and opened up. A release, not a counterweight or an impeding force—it does not all have to come down to one thing.

Grief Work

In the early morning
he listens
by the window,
makes
the first utterance
and tries to overhear
himself
say something
from which
in that silence
it is impossible to retreat.

—from "The Poet"
by DAVID WHYTE

. . . it is not intended . . . that any other should know
intellectually what, known but intellectually, would be for
his injury—what knowing intellectually, he would imagine
he had grasped, perhaps even appropriated . . . It is not a
fruit or a jewel to be stored, but a well springing by the
wayside.

—from *Unspoken Sermons*
by GEORGE MACDONALD

What exactly was so unappealing to me about the terms *grief management* and *grief work*? Granted, difficult, complex things demand management and work. I suspected formulaic advice, and my energy for potentially disappointing directions was limited. When I browsed through "how to grieve" books and "basic grief skills" manuals, they left me alone, delivered nothing that stayed. Grief has weight. Much of the writing about "handling" it did not. There were too many stepladders of the stages of grief, framed by quotes and butterflies and flowers, and there was not enough poetry. No rancid rage, no bitter phrases, no companions in my choking despair, no depth and breadth to keep me company in my sorrow's labyrinths. Too much in these books was antiseptic and distancing and sometimes moving too quickly to the light, the redemption, the blessing in the pain. "Says *who*?" I cried or screamed at different times.

At the same time, I was not keen on selling out to a life trimmed in morose black, a graying eking out in a monotonous palette of somber and pallid and grim, or a futile maze of convoluted grief. I had the added motivation of Ike's prodding and his understandable questioning, his dependence on me for a sizable portion of the sorting out of what was happening to him and what was to be made of it.

He was no longer depending on me for the daily things. Soltane coworkers and companions were doing that in a way that allowed him, often forced him, to continue to open beyond himself. For all of us, I needed to leave no stone unturned. Cynicism was too costly. So I signed up for a grief workshop—"skills-based," the promotional material said— and resolved to approach it with an open mind.

In attendance were counselors and chaplains and individuals who had recently lost loved ones. There were some interesting charts outlining the leader's main points. The United States is a loss-denying society. Using the word *died* is healthier than *passed*. There are six major types of loss. Ours with Ike filled the bill in all categories—material, relationship, functional, role, systemic, and intrapsychic. I heard that loss accumulates, that every individual has a loss history, that others' losses can be a mirror to my own, that if I forgo my own grief work, I will not be able to see others' grief but will be stuck in mine.

Okay, they had my attention. What *is* grief work? What *are* the skills? The workshop leader deferred my questions. She wanted me to experience something other than hearing her answer my question, something other than *a fruit or a jewel to be stored . . . grasped . . . appropriated.*

We started with a personal loss self-inventory and continued with six definitions of grief, descriptions of grief and its behavioral, physical, emotional, cognitive, and spiritual reactions. I was beginning to feel a bit hedged in, and when we started with metaphors for grief and theories of grief, I was definitely thinking more about lunch. But then a Vietnam-vet-now-prison-counselor, in asking a question, told his story. He works with convicted criminals toward making peace with the shock of their own guilt—his and theirs, he said—with the horrible awareness of what each had been capable of doing given certain circumstances. Hearing him, grief and loss resumed a fullness and weight, more multi-faceted than I had previously considered. In this widened, expanded grief, my particular shred found a place. The *well springing by the wayside* for me had come in this veteran-counselor's story, in his utterance of *something / from which / in that silence / it is impossible to retreat.*

His story and those of others since stay with me. In their presence, there is room again. Grief is not a zero-sum game. I can begin to pick up pieces even as I lay others down. My grief work is not so much about climbing a ladder to get out of it as it is about the awareness of how many people are in it with me.

Holding Patterns

. . .

My anguished spirit, like a bird,
Beating against my lips I heard;
Yet lay the weight so close about
There was no room for it without.
And so beneath the weight lay I
And suffered death, but could not die.

. . .

I know not how such things can be;
I only know there came to me
A fragrance such as never clings
To aught save happy living things;
A sound as of some joyous elf
Singing sweet songs to please himself,
And, through and over everything,
A sense of glad awakening.

The grass, a-tiptoe at my ear,
Whispering to me I could hear;
I felt the rain's cool finger-tips
Brushed tenderly across my lips,
Laid gently on my sealèd sight,
And all at once the heavy night
Fell from my eyes and I could see,—
A drenched and dripping apple-tree,
A last long line of silver rain,
A sky grown clear and blue again.
And as I looked a quickening gust
Of wind blew up to me and thrust
Into my face a miracle
Of orchard-breath, and with the smell,—
I know not how such things can be!—
I breathed my soul back into me.

—from "Renascence"
by Edna St. Vincent Millay

———

Poems have become
a safe house where we meet
and you sometimes find
the manuscript of our endeavors
illuminated by mind light.

Or, paper bridges, they reach
between felt and spoken,

a gulf freight must cross
to reach the trade routes of said.

Among the cargo is passion
gift-wrapped in words.
Bon bons and bon mots.
Of late, we sample them
less often, and I miss
their secret tidings and gripes.

Wittgenstein quipped:
"What can't be said can't be said
and can't be whistled either."
Yet one can hear all
the vowels of the wind,
a short account of longing,
as they whistle through
the veils of a poem.

—from "A Short Account of Longing"
by DIANE ACKERMAN

*T*he fall and winter months five years into Ike's illness brought with them change. After a trial visit, Ike moved from Maple Hill in New Hampshire to Camphill Soltane, where he took readily to the larger population of young people. By mid-winter, Nick knew where he would be headed for college the next fall, and Noah and I had found the apartment in New York to which we would move when Nick graduated from high school.

Noah's father had died the previous spring, and Noah was sad and a little lost. Nick had a prolonged bout with migraines and a severe case of senioritis. Taking what they both said they wanted and helping to make it happen, I had fueled the college application process and our move. Where had this energy come from?

I needed to step back and let be. If the lying full *beneath the weight* in Edna St. Vincent Millay's poem had figured into some turning for me, had *breathed my soul back into me*, I needed to allow them—Noah and Nick—even free fall. The coming alive for those with whom my life is bound up requires unbinding.

That unbinding leaves a weight to be held. A weight of longing for it to be better, closer to resolution, if not with Ike's illness, then with something—our marriage, Nick's goals, our work. In this unmet yearning, *Poems have become / a safe house* for holding still *between felt and spoken* with *passion / gift-wrapped in words*.

These yearning times huddle, begging, around the periods of intense sorrow. In these beggar moments, I imagine myself toes on a threshold, pulling to me the centrifugal forces of my longings. The fragments—*be, hold, long*— emerge and assemble themselves in a horizontally elongated diamond diagram—*be*, *behold*, and *hold* across the top; *be*, *long*, and *belong* across the bottom.

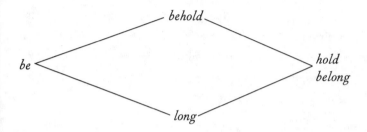

The far right side is where I yearn to be—to hold and be held and to belong. Movement in this diagram is from left to right, but arriving at the right side is not easy or guaranteed. The *be* at the left is not laid-back, but seized and intentional, what C. K. Williams has called a *violent awareness*. Shocked awake, with minimal denial. Not everyone wants to go there. Many times I do not. Beholding is a matter of choice and will, an effortful choosing to see. I see loss, incompleteness, hurt, aloneness, and limitations. When I can hold on to the things beheld—many of which ache to hold, ask to be buried and forgotten—a staying-in-place comes, a centered holding. If it weren't for the bottom half of the diamond, this endpoint might seem attenuated and dismal.

The warm, flowing undercurrents of the lower side propel me. They are other-generated. Longings deliver grace; they arise. Yearnings for knowledge or health or love or stability or assurance or connection or touch or relief come on their own. Fueled by exogenous injections, they are the engine of the whole affair. The commonality, the humanness of longing allows belonging, seen and received, not earned.

I try to hold steady and lie full *beneath the weight* and await *a quickening gust / Of wind . . . all / the vowels of the wind, / a short account of longing, / as they whistle through / the veils of a poem.* A way there and a place, to be held and to belong, mediated by words.

Body

CARTOGRAPHY

As you lay in sleep
I saw the chart
Of artery and vein
Running from your heart,

Plain as the strength
Marked upon the leaf
Along the length,
Mortal and brief,

Of your gaunt hand.
I saw it clear:
The wiry brand
Of the life we bear

Mapped like the great
Rivers that rise
Beyond our fate
And distant from our eyes

—LOUISE BOGAN

───────

. . . *What you called* that yearning.

What you finally gave up. We want the spring to come
    and the winter to pass. We want
whoever to call or not call, a letter, a kiss—we want
    more and more and then more of it.
But there are moments, walking, when I catch a
    glimpse of myself in the window glass,
say, the window of the corner video store, and I'm
    gripped by a cherishing so deep

for my own blowing hair, chapped face, and unbuttoned
    coat that I'm speechless:
I am living, I remember you.

—from *What the Living Do*
by MARIE HOWE

*L*ike some malevolent baker or pastry chef, Ike's illness has patted down, thinned out, and rolled over parts of his body, reshaping and misshaping his feet, arching his spine, thrusting his abdomen forward, smoothing away the convolutions in his brain. Things meant to be firm soften. Once-pliable muscles petrify. Things meant to move become rigid. Legs trying to lie still tremble and shake the mattress. His body washes from itself what, in another body, is kept. Essential building blocks take leave.

Since the first appearance of each of my children, I have found loving them physically, bodily, to be irresistible. Holding, cuddling, cradling, wrestling, romping, snuggling, hugging—at different stages, these are the sweet feel to me of mothering. I have even loved most of their bodies' particular smells. When they were younger, I knew their physical selves almost instinctually, my hand detecting a fever as accurately as the thermometer. My back rubs were requested on into self-conscious adolescence.

In the early months of Ike's illness, I would awaken at night and move quietly to his bedroom to listen to his breathing, to scout for night tremors, excessive drooling, other indicators of degeneration. I did not disturb Ike or Noah or Nick. Sometimes I was disturbed by what I saw. Yet, staring at illness in the dark, I also saw my son sleeping, the pleasure of that. I enjoy it still. In the weeks he is with me, on holiday from Soltane, I look in on him sleeping and smile to see how he occupies the space on his bed. Watching sleeping children may be parenthood's great treat. The specific, my own sons, opens out to the general, perhaps universal. *The wiry brand / Of the life we bear / Mapped like the great / Rivers that rise / Beyond our fate / And distant from our eyes.*

As Ike sustains less intellectual connection, I reach past the inherent sadness of his body's changes. I cannot reject his body changed by this illness, abandon the field in which it is playing out. When I embrace him, I hold his illness and feel his continued hold on life pushing back against what is lost. When I do not see him for a while, I miss his physicality as much as anything, the way he lurches, grabs doorjambs, holds and jerks my shoulder when we walk together, as if he is yanking his life to him with each effortful step, tiresome and precious. Donald Hall in "Ardor" speaks of caring for his wife, Jane Kenyon.

Nursing her I felt alive
in the animal moment,
scenting the predator.
Her death was the worst thing
that could happen,
and caring for her was best.

Alive / in the animal moment, the body tells me, in the way the body can, that life continues, in Ike's, in mine. The incarnation is not done. Seeing his will to live awakens mine, as his loss has mine.

For years I had been looking for mental routes to some relief in this sadness, through intellectually working things out, expecting an occasional epiphany, like a bright idea, a cerebral lightbulb. I had not considered that healing might come more in the form of a surge of physical energy. I began to picture a diminutive insurgent body rebelling against the superpower intellect. Bringing snippets of relief and reprieve, the body—Ike's, mine—has cried out with . . . *What you called* that yearning.

Marie Howe's poem reminds me that life in its physical is specific, that I live in details, in *blowing hair, chapped face, and unbuttoned coat,* even when I catch only the occasional glimpse. The reflection caught recharges the yearning, and I *want more and more and then more of it . . . a cherishing so deep / . . . that I'm speechless.* I live and love in the particular, and poetry holds me in context and in connection with things beyond and general.

Death is the body's ultimate function. Illness and disability are preambles, rehearsals. Living, too, honors the gone-before—individuals, Marie Howe's brother, former abilities, Ike's reasoning. *I am living, I remember you.* In claiming the physical Ike, his particularities and specifics, the illness returns to human size. It does not take over; Ike and I can take it in. I can cherish trembling knees and curved feet, the coarse texture of his hair, the firmness of his arms. To love the sick body goes against the grain. I am intentional about it. I think of Ike's first baby shoes, aqua-green high-tops with red circles on the outside of each an-kle, and his current high-tops, worn down in rolled-over, crooked ways. Not a saccharine reflection or futile nostal-gia, I willfully connect the two through the physical. The same feet of the same individual filled the shoes twenty years apart as surely as my father once wore combat boots. We are our physical selves, and we are not, and both are true.

A GREEN CRAB'S SHELL

Not, exactly, green:
closer to bronze
preserved in kind brine,

something retrieved
from a Greco-Roman wreck,
patinated and oddly

muscular. We cannot
know what his fantastic
legs were like—

though evidence
suggests eight
complexly folded

scuttling works
of armament, crowned
by the foreclaws'

gesture of menace
and power. A gull's
gobbled the center,

leaving this chamber
—size of a demitasse—
open to reveal

a shocking, Giotto blue.
Though it smells
of seaweed and ruin,

this little traveling case
comes with such lavish lining!
Imagine breathing

surrounded by
the brilliant rinse
of summer's firmament.

What color is
the underside of skin?
Not so bad, to die,

if we could be opened
into this—
if the smallest chambers

of ourselves,
similarly,
revealed some sky.

—MARK DOTY

Barbara Lane had Lou Gehrig's disease. I knew her for the last eighteen months of her life; a relative said I should have known her before. She amazed me. She showed me how to die and how to live until she did, facing each aspect of her body closing down and shutting off. She lived and died in the particularities. As her illness advanced, her physical beauty collected itself and drew back into round eyes; her clear, caring expressiveness floating on the surface; and long, graceful fingers, lovely even as they no longer obeyed her wishes. I can barely imagine how her body pained her. She occupied it faithfully, in the particular physical details, her lovely silk pajamas, rings on her fingers. At the same time, Barbara always suggested something beyond. I may have thought I was there with my friend only to adjust the customized computer mouse she operated with her elbow to push out letter by letter what she needed to say in her last eighteen months. I was also there for what I saw in her eyes: *Rivers that rise / Beyond our fate.*

Mark Doty's poem puts specific, physical beauty in the rotting, gull-ravaged remains of a crab, and a *little traveling case / comes with such lavish lining!* Perhaps in our tiniest secluded parts, under our skin, in the husks we leave behind—centers gobbled, armaments and all signs of menace and power gone—is *the brilliant rinse / of summer's firmament / . . . some sky.* The body sung into, incarnate incantation.

Rocking

And oh, my love, as I rock for you to-night,
And have not any longer any hope
To heal the suffering, or make requite
For all your life of asking and despair,
I own that some of me is dead to-night

—from "The End"
by D. H. LAWRENCE

*B*oth of my sons loved being rocked when they were little. In 1976, when Granny Fay, my father's mother,
died, I inherited among other things a green rocking chair
from her large wraparound screened porch. The rocking
chair reminded me of that wide porch, where she would
visit with folks much of the temperate North Carolina year.

She always sat in one of the wicker chairs with cushions; I preferred the smooth, slat-bottom, cane-back rockers with no cushions and long rockers for wide, smooth rides. Her grandchildren's boyfriends and girlfriends, the serious contenders and the just-passing-through, were routinely photographed in rockers on that porch. Granny Fay was passionate and jolly and loved to take pictures. Memories of her continue to fill me; many are situated in the rockers on that porch.

The green rocker endured an apartment balcony in northern Virginia and an exposed patio behind a row house in southeast D.C. to hold me by the bay window in our second-floor Brooklyn Heights apartment when we brought Ike home from the hospital in 1982. It went on with us to our first house in New Jersey, where Nick was born, in 1985, and it migrated with the seasons from the living room to the side porch. It had a high back and wide, flat arms, key for those middle-of-the-night feedings and rockings when the baby stayed awake longer than the person holding him.

A couple of years ago Nick and I were in New Jersey, in the town where he was born and where his grandfather, Noah's father, had just died. Arriving after the end of a semester-away program, Nick had missed by a day being able to speak with Gramps. He and I were on our way to the orchard and farmers' market a few miles from Gramps' and G'ma's home, a favorite destination for apple cider or fruit or pies. This particular day, Nick and I went also for some time for just the two of us. I had missed him, and we were all missing Gramps. Usually lively and talkative, Nick was quiet. On the way to the orchard, a long curve sweeping just short of a complete circle skirts a grassy, unused field.

"Look!" Nick pointed to the center of the field. Barely visible in the tall May grass and weeds was a rocking chair. "That is so cool."

I agreed—to think that someone would sit there and rock, and what they would see, and that they would take the time to.

Rocking and comfort.

On Sunday afternoon circuits to visit both sets of grand-parents, in the months when it was too cool for the porch, my mother would regularly sit in one particular platform rocker in Granny Fay's living room. It was a carved ma-hogany velvet-upholstered chair, low, and comfortable for my mother's short legs. Granny Fay designated it my mother's special chair the same way the pecan pie was my older brother's, the coconut pie my younger brother's, the cinnamon-swirl bread mine, the Hershey's Kisses in the candy dish my mother's, the iced tea my father's. She con-nected people with objects. She showed her caring that way. My mother's special rocker from Granny Fay now sits in her own living room. I think of Granny Fay and her way of caring and rocking and comfort.

A friend of Ike's from his months at Maple Hill in New Hampshire does not stand still. He rocks front to back, one foot to the other. Rocking is not uncommon among people with some disabilities. Around them, I want to rock. It seems a more normal, appealing state than not rocking. I often think of rocking when I run.

Rocking moves; it is a dynamic. I inch toward the possibility of living and moving without a full understanding of what is going on with Ike. Leading with the body rather than the head, it is a gradual, permeable process, an osmosis—back and forth, not all or nothing.

Comfort is "with strength," to make strong; it is not obliteration of all suffering. A *life of asking and despair, / . . . some of me is dead to-night*, but only some, and in the context of loving and rocking.

Shipwreck

I AM

I am—yet what I am, none cares or knows;
My friends forsake me like a memory lost:
I am the self-consumer of my woes—
They rise and vanish in oblivion's host
Like shadows in love-frenzied stifled throes—
And yet I am, and live—like vapours toss't

Into the nothingness of scorn and noise,
Into the living sea of waking dreams
Where there is neither sense of life or joys
But the vast shipwreck of my life's esteems;
Even the dearest that I love the best
Are strange—nay, rather, stranger than the rest.

I long for scenes where man hath never trod,
A place where woman never smiled nor wept,
There to abide with my Creator, God,
And sleep as I in childhood sweetly slept,
Untroubling and untroubled where I lie,
The grass below—above, the vaulted sky.

—JOHN CLARE

Ike's illness showed up when he was fourteen, smack-dab in Erikson's "competency" stage, Piaget's "abstract operational." I worried that Ike's sense of self and his illness might have become inextricably intertwined. He might not have grasped a self-perception apart from "sick," and that seemed unhealthy and unfair. His therapist suggested that Ike choose a name for his illness to remind him that it was "other," to provide a distance. He named the illness Larry, who knows why? In recent years, the name Larry has rarely been mentioned. About his aches, pains, fears, and limitations, mostly he has said "I."

Identity is not all clarity but consists also of gray areas and parts that ease into focus, then fade and resurface. When Ike's illness appeared, he was not armed with a steady perception of nuance or subtlety. With its assault, his world moved quickly toward rote. He would get a bare-bones understanding without perceiving the whole shape of the flesh, and his far-flung dreams were rarely tied to a chance in a blue moon. In spite of his growing slowness and difficulty in moving, he would persist in telling people that he wished to be an emergency rescue worker.

My self-perception incorporates so much of who I *wish* I were—dreams, illusions, delusions, self-deceptions. Some I need, temporarily, partially, until I am ready to discard them. In my fifty years, with my generous share of mistakes, I have grown quite attached to blurring the line between "I am" and "I think I am." More than hard evidence objectively analyzed, my self is swaddled in a palatable cushion, some half-truths if not untruths—benign, I hope—to be peeled away and tossed as I am able. This is not Ike's luxury. Since he has less awareness and less flexibility than most, Ike's life is often asking him to come to terms with his limits, limits no one would want to see.

With a twisted kindness, his illness is insulating the pain of self-perception with muddled awareness. As he loses pieces, the *vast shipwreck of* [his] *life's esteems* becomes more the destruction of the visions held by those who love him— the shape of the lifeboat we had hoped for him.

John Clare's poem begins *I am*, a declaration of existence, a determined statement of being. His being is in despair and in isolation from humans, but not from God. The poem gives order in three stanzas of six lines each and strong rhymes—*knows, woes, throes, lost, toss't, noise, joys, dreams, esteems, best, rest, trod, God, wept, slept, lie, sky*. As confined and contained as an unglossed, well-defined identity, the poem does not run misery pell-mell all over the page. It ends lying on the grass looking up at the sky. With *frenzied*, *vapours*, *nothingness*, *neither sense of life or joys*, there is sure being.

In this poem, *My friends forsake*, and *I long for scenes where man hath never trod*. Distance grows and is sought—a reasonable response, after all. In the words of Jimmy Cox's song, as recorded by Eric Clapton, "nobody knows you when you're down and out." Sometimes I especially want separation from those I love most. Close friends and family best know the plans of the trip not to be taken and will recognize in detail *the vast shipwreck*. They will know most particularly the hurt and sadness, and I theirs for me. I long, if only temporarily, for a secluded place.

A place apart, short of abandoning the self. Turning away to lie down completely alone in a field and say and know "I am," where maybe God—the great "I am"— abides: this is the power of this poem. Ike is who he is in spite of losses and unknowing. I can resolve to be *the self-consumer of my woes* and work to avoid the reverse. A ship has wrecked, broken apart. Floating fragments, each worthy of things hoped for, worked for, not awarded, not attained, not received, friends, myself, bob by.

Surprises

———————

On the lawn of memory,
      violets suddenly appear: each a sensation

like a note, but without the dirge of loss,
      translucent, welcome, unexpected.

Photo albums open their leaves
      with a calm that seems phenomenal.

Tonight the sun reclines in the sky,
      and time is a kneeling animal.

—from "Grace"
by DIANE ACKERMAN

———————

SUNSET

Slowly the west reaches for clothes of new colors
which it passes to a row of ancient trees.
You look, and soon these two worlds both leave you,
one part climbs toward heaven, one sinks to earth,

leaving you, not really belonging to either,
not so hopelessly dark as that house that is silent,
not so unswervingly given to the eternal as that thing
that turns to a star each night and climbs—

leaving you (it is impossible to untangle the threads)
your own life, timid and standing high and growing,
so that, sometimes blocked in, sometimes reaching out,
one moment your life is a stone in you, and the next,
     a star.

—RAINER MARIA RILKE
(translated by Robert Bly)

*Y*ou may be surprised at this. I was. About 6:30 on an
April Sunday morning, I awoke, the bright sun re-
flecting off the snow and into my window of the house on
the hill above Bellows Falls, Vermont. I started the coffee
and made the circuit of windows, looking long out of each

in the stillness before Ike arose, as I did each morning in our two weeks there. From the bathroom window on the west side of the house, I saw it. Perhaps a hundred yards away, a large orange-tan cat looked first to its left and then loped over the crest of the hill and out of sight. Had I been standing next to it, I estimated it would have reached to my hip. My first thought was "lion," like the ones I had seen in Africa. My second thought was, This is Vermont. You're out of your mind. Get a cup of coffee.

The sighting came unanticipated. I had read no tracking books and had focused little on what wildlife I might encounter in our two weeks there. Later in the day, I noticed a few tracks, but other sights and duties took my attention elsewhere. People doubted that I had seen what I claimed. The mountain lion (or "catamount," as the man at the bookstore called it) disappeared from most of New England during the 1940s. Recently, scientists have been hearing reports of sightings. This hill in Vermont abuts 250 acres of natural area. A typical mountain lion requires a range of 175 square miles. That the scientists doubted me mattered little. The beauty of the surprise still lingers.

Surprise means to be taken over, overtaken. Unexpected and unsought, it happens to advantage and disadvantage. So filled at times with the bad, I can find it difficult to squeeze in the good. A surprise can inject the good swiftly. Even if the aftermath of the surprise is the "okay, maybe that wasn't a mountain lion" of reasonableness, the wide-eyed "but it could have been" of wonder remains. Wonder holds the space, a placeholder regardless. Poems can surprise like *violets* [that] *suddenly appear: each a sensation / like a note, but without the dirge of loss, / translucent, welcome, unexpected.* Surprises, with pure, clear rings, come from a direction entirely other than laments. They can overtake and change what I thought I knew, *clothes of new colors*, the *stone in you, . . . next, a star.*

Sensory Illness

INTRODUCTION TO POETRY

I ask them to take a poem
and hold it up to the light
like a color slide

or press an ear against its hive.

I say drop a mouse into a poem
and watch him probe his way out,

or walk inside the poem's room
and feel the walls for a light switch.

I want them to water-ski
across the surface of a poem
waving at the author's name on the shore.

But all they do
is tie the poem to a chair with rope
and torture a confession out of it.

They begin beating it with a hose
to find out what it really means.

—BILLY COLLINS

Take the illness and hold it up to the light like a color slide—the spastic paraparesis, the dementia, the hematological abnormality (MGUS). What do they look like? Can the light get through? At times not, as if the slide were poorly developed or I were trying to focus through bleary eyes. At times, yes, and the colors of the paraparesis are stark and bold—reds and blues and purples. The dementia, more faded around the edges, less completely filled in, torn swatches of tie-dyed fabric—I remember the T-shirts he dyed his first summer at sleepaway camp. The MGUS snaking in red across the ground of the other two, there, interlaced, affecting but not creating a whole.

Pressing my ear against the illness's hive. What is its sound? The sound of hard breathing, because it is much harder for him to move than it is for me. The sound of a heart squeezing ninety beats a minute after a walk of five feet to the nurses' station. So why did you think he was tired all of a sudden in the middle of the afternoon when you had planned other things you thought he would especially enjoy? Or needed to do? Did you think? Did you listen? Always there are at least two sounds when you listen—the yearning to live and the illness—the first a steady beat; the other, a muffling sound, vying for attention.

Sometimes his illness is the irregular ka-thump . . . ka-ka-thump, sha-thump of his heavy, then sliding, irregular footfalls, with unexpected pauses interspersed. The sounds of falls—the clump-bump-ping of knees, hips, cane hitting the wooden floor. Ping-ping-ping-pinging down to silence when the fall is on the concrete sidewalk. No cries, no curses. The damned thing endures. The illness survives on and on, unrelenting, dependable. Laugh sounds invade. Ike's drawn-out laugh with its exaggerated inhale finale evokes a small gasoline-powered engine having trouble starting. The sound of his younger brother laughing back and then all of us joining in—laughing at the sound of laughing, almost choking at dinner one night when we got so tickled. Where did *that* come from?

Ike's illness is a mouse hemmed in by glue boards. Squealing and straining, writhing for its very existence; then caught, it flirts, seduces life to pull over for a little while in a secluded spot. No dumb mouse, he knows about the drowning bucket. Forget the light switch, he squeaks. We can learn to live in this gray.

Waterskiing over the surface of this illness, we hit huge bumps, are sent sky-high, look ridiculous. But we are still on skis. The boat whips us every which way. For a moment we pride ourselves that we are gaining experience, that we will improve the next time over these rough spots, but we never do. No two times around are ever quite the same.

Is the *author's name on the shore* a spectator watching the sporting event, or is he eyewitness to an approaching disaster? Is that dread or curiosity or enjoyment beneath his dark glasses? Surely not boredom or disinterest, is it? He *is* staying with us, isn't he? Waving back to us? Who is it, anyway, the author of this illness?

We confess, we have beat up the poor illness many times. Tied it down with ten-kilo weights of lab reports and strips of insurance tape, beat it around the head with the rubber hoses of repeated MRIs, twenty-four-hour urine collections, electrophosphoresis, skin-muscle biopsies, enzyme studies, CSF exams, SSEPs.

We release you, but you are already unleashed. In him. We meet you there. Your turf? His, too. His eyes and ears and nose and mouth and hands. What will you have us know? Will we be dazzled? By you? By your complexity? By a yearning to live?

Shelving Selves

The world
was whole because
it shattered. When it shattered,
then we knew what it was.

It never healed itself.
But in the deep fissures, smaller worlds appeared:
. . .

Tributaries
feeding into a large river: I had
many lives . . .

I had many lives. Feeding
into a river, the river
feeding into a great ocean. If the self
becomes invisible has it disappeared?

. . .

I had lives before this, stems
of a spray of flowers: they became
one thing, held by a ribbon at the center, a ribbon
visible under the hand. Above the hand,
the branching future, stems
ending in flowers. And the gripped fist—
that would be the self in the present.

—from "Formaggio"
by LOUISE GLÜCK

*I*n the fourth year of his illness and his tenth week of college, Ike was asked to take a medical leave. The night of his most panicked unraveling, Ike would not be talked down from his fears. All I could do was to keep him company on the phone, repeating whatever calming, reassuring words I could locate. Noah flew up to collect him the next morning while I taught a full day at school, gave notice yet again of my need to take a leave, and then hosted a dinner party for twenty friends, fibbing that Noah had been called away unexpectedly "on business." At the time I saw no alternative. Dividing the work, putting a pleasant face on things, Noah using vacation days for short-term crises, and my taking leaves from teaching for the longer-haul concerns—these had become standard features in our coping with Ike's illness.

The poem erupts at the beginning. *The world / was whole because / it shattered. When it shattered, / then we knew what it was.* A revelation predicated on an obliteration. *In the deep fissures*, small worlds appear; in them, new selves. "Formaggio" brings the multiplicity of a market day, bouquets of flowers and shop-lined streets, the fishmonger, the fruit. The bouquet is a spray of flowers tied gently with a ribbon, an attractive array, a collection that goes together—all the daily functional roles, the wished-for roles, and the ones temporarily obscured. *And the gripped fist— / that would be the self in the present*, is more wanted, more urgent than the kind ribbon, and risks strangling *the branching future, stems / ending in flowers* before getting to water. *I had many lives*, the poem repeats.

Every human role is composed of multiple, disparate sliver roles. Being the mother of a sick son is no exception. Seeing the slivers helps me, keeping tabs on the ones that make me uncomfortable and the ones I slide into seamlessly, noticing when one is giving way to another, when one is surrendering and another emerging, when one or two may have been locked in sustained combat, when a role or a sliver threatens to become me. Seeing them, taking note, I can try to avoid becoming my functions. It does not always work. Some of the roles have been more important than any "me," at least in the short term. Of course, I would have traded all the "me's" I could muster for an end to what was happening to Ike.

With a chronically and progressively ill son, among the

more demanding roles have been those requiring "doctor-speak," presenting the case to physicians knowledgeably but not so intensely as to threaten or suggest excess concern and risk being perceived as demanding or difficult, with the possible result that Ike's issues might not receive their due. To be taken seriously has demanded combinations of knowledge, patience, organization, and charm. Hard-to-diagnose cases are time-consuming, with little promise of return on the investment for the doctor. An element of selling the case, making a pitch for the doctor's focused involvement, dances around the edges of most first-time appointments. With subsequent visits, this aspect resurfaces—is he/she still with us? Have they given this any thought since our last visit? Why should they?

It is odd trying to coax doctors to be deeply invested in an isolated, difficult case, to care about Ike close to as much as I do, to find it sufficiently interesting to pursue vigorously, to dig in, to consider beyond. Many of the doctors have had their own motivation, personal commitment, and best intentions; some who had it in the beginning ran out of it over time. What human being would not find tiresome the seventh e-mail in two months requesting the results of the test for an extremely rare disorder that is not likely, mathematically or clinically speaking, to be the answer, and for which treatment is, at best, experimental? Surely there are more promising matters on which to focus, and the preference for them over the obscure and remote makes sense. What is there to say to someone who has been waiting for

Niemann-Pick Type C results for eight months because one lab botched the test twice? Many talented, kind, well-meaning people would reasonably avoid these communications. I have known that, but I have also been convinced that following through as persistently and politely as I could on every suggested test was the responsible thing to do as Ike's mother and advocate.

With this responsibility, maybe the self that was shelved or the sliver that was shed was the spontaneous, fun-loving self. Prone to consider life a subject for study, I became even more dedicated to that route once Ike got sick. Everything needed thinking through, options warranted weighing, records and results needed scrutinizing. Life in our home became too often a problem to be solved. Long on contemplation, I shortchanged life on the living end.

Yet spontaneity and fun, infrequent guests when things are precarious and infused with sadness, have raised their heads. Recently they are just out there, with a different texture, perhaps even a richer feel, than they would have if Ike were not sick. The hopeful sliver of me is slipping back in, and the working-so-hard-at-it and the mourning slivers are edging over, a little at least.

A tentative stance; things can tumble quickly the other way. Recently a flurry of doctors' e-mails—negotiating precisely what tests to have done on what tissue stored where, or whether to take new tissue and how, and what lab to send it to—called up in me that familiar alert urgency. Until resolved, over several days, the exchange with the doctors overshadowed all. I participated, even occasionally correcting and redirecting. I am certainly no medical expert, but I am the Ike expert. No one knows his case, in the overall sense, as encyclopedically as I—what has been tried and looked for and what not yet. It has seemed a mother's job. But who was I to spout off eleven-syllable names of rare diseases or to suggest that tissues frozen in 1997 were probably only marginally viable in 2003? Don't I know my place? No. Frankly, in this unknown and changing world of medicine confronting me, I often do not know my place. And as it reshapes, I again seek footing.

Advocating for Ike in these interactions with medical professionals takes precedence over everything else I do during that time. My sense of myself becomes the outcome of the particular exchange with the doctors. My work, my thinking, my schedule, my friendships and family relationships are pushed back in the line. For the first four years I could put Ike's illness and my part of the management of the diagnostic search out of my mind during the school day while I was teaching. Students exited at the end of the day, and Ike's concerns entered, but there was balance and hard work. I loved my job and found great pleasure among my colleagues and students. Once the hematological and cognitive components crept in and the urgency level shot up, the balance was less tenable.

People at church extended profound kindness. Several

friends knew how to care and let be. They were not of-
fended by my kicking, squirming, screaming sadness. But I
seemed to lose almost completely what limited ability I had
had for small talk, and I became for many, I am sure, a
"heavy." As we moved into the sixth year of Ike's illness,
I bided time and prayed for Nick's graduation so that we
could move to the next thing, a new home for us, a base of
support closer to Ike.

Spontaneous and sociable slivers of my self have been
shelved, at least partially, and not without loss. I am precarious, fragile, and fearful of imposing. What friend would
want me with all my sad baggage? At the same time, I do
not want always to live on the sidelines. I do not care to become a professional loner.

Some new selves are introducing themselves. A stronger
voice, born of the necessity of speaking for Ike and reworked inside contemplation and living, is beginning to
speak my views, my thoughts, my opinions. I am held by a
deep and profound attentiveness to my life and those in it
who will let me care passionately about them. These things
are blessings, some of them brought forth and nurtured by
the process of living with this illness, some by the people
who have cared for Ike in New Hampshire and in Pennsylvania. Especially are they teaching me to savor intentional-
ity. As disabilities mount, spontaneity is difficult, sometimes
counter-indicated. Planning with care, not anxiety, can prepare a field where the spontaneous might sprout.

One self feels essentially like resistance, a refusal to submit. Reached and held, this one can be strength among so many slivers that are accommodating and placating and being what others need me to be. Sometimes the more pacifist pieces of me fence the resistance in and label it a trouble-maker, shut it out. An energy source, it fights back.

In a recent British movie, a woman grieving the loss of her husband hears from her son, who is trying to manage her and get back to his own life, "Now, Mum, be reasonable."

"Why?" she turns to him and asks.

"What do you mean *'why?'* Mum?" The son is perplexed.

"Why must I be reasonable?" his mother asks. "What if I feel like being completely *un*reasonable? What's wrong with that?" And in the course of the film, she is a strong-headed and highly unconventional new widow. She defies traditional notions of "appropriate behavior" under the circumstances, and with energy, she seeks life's uncertainties before certain death.

Maybe the feisty rebel sliver is the staying alive, the part that reminds me in the gut that I am not Ike's illness, just as he is not. Memorials to what has been can be visited; moving in to stay is not an option.

DELTA

If you have taken this rubble for my past
raking through it for fragments you could sell

know that I long ago moved on
deeper into the heart of the matter

If you think you can grasp me, think again:
my story flows in more than one direction
a delta springing from the riverbed
with its five fingers spread

—ADRIENNE RICH

In *raking* and in a *delta springing from the riverbed* is humus, the once-living matter that enriches the earth. Many experiences, lives, selves, often unnoticed, work into the soil of my life and feed me. Held and released. In the *gripped fist* and the *five fingers spread*.

A multislivered self is a bit different from the integrated self, which, as a sort of enforcer, marshals disparate roles into a sensible whole.

Actually, it would embarrass me to be told that more than a
single self is a kind of disease. I've had, in my time, more
than I could possibly count or keep track of . . . Five years
ago I was another person, juvenile, doing and saying things I
couldn't possibly agree with now. Ten years ago I was a
stranger. Twenty-forty years ago . . . I've forgotten. The only
thing close to what you might call illness, in my experience
was in the gaps in the queue when one had finished and left

the place before the next one was ready to start, and there
was nobody around at all . . .

To be truthful there have been a few times when they were all
there at once . . .

What do we meet about? It is hard to say. The door bangs
open and in they come, calling for the meeting to start, and
then they all talk at once . . .

—from "The Selves"
by LEWIS THOMAS

In another essay in the same book, *The Medusa and the
Snail*, Thomas writes of Montaigne. "He was fascinated by
his own inconstancy, and came to believe that inconsistency
is an identifying biological characteristic of human beings
in general. 'We are all patchwork,' he says, 'so shapeless and
diverse in composition that each bit, each moment, plays its
own game.' "

The words of these poets and essayists have given me a
self that is a bouquet of flowers, a spreading delta, a queue
of selves waiting, a gap in the line, a disputatious committee
meeting, and a patchwork. I have the permission when
things are broken to give myself a break. Some selves are
received; some I can kick into being with help and persistence. I can follow up with the medical lab, coaxing and ca-

joling and making sure the test they do this time is for cholestanol and not cholesterol, and I can run to a me that is not focused on the illness and its monitoring. The self laid down one day to pursue medical test records has not been abandoned, but can be picked up the next day. I have not become immutably, irretrievably other because of the demands of the day, or the demands of the illness.

In 1878 and 1879, the novelist and fantasy writer George MacDonald lost two of his children to illness: Mary in her twenties, Maurice, fifteen. Mourning deeply, MacDonald worked on. In the following year, he wrote a verse for each day of the year, collected in his *Diary of an Old Soul*. His entry for October 10 reads, in part,

> *With every morn my life afresh must break*
> *The crust of self . . .*
> *That thy wind-spirit may rush in . . .*

The day, the fresh wind, the me's waiting.

Without the Loneliness

It might be lonelier
Without the Loneliness—
I'm so accustomed to my Fate—
Perhaps the Other—Peace—

Would interrupt the Dark—
And crowd the little Room—
Too scant—by Cubits—to contain
The Sacrament—of Him—

I am not used to Hope—
It might intrude upon—
Its sweet parade—blaspheme the place—
Ordained to Suffering—

It might be easier
To fail—with Land in Sight—

Than gain——My Blue Peninsula——
To perish——of Delight——

                              ——EMILY DICKINSON, #405

*A*n endurance poem for anyone with eyes adjusted to
seeing in the dark, *not used to Hope—— / . . . Ordained
to Suffering*, for one who can trace the shape of a sorrow
from the inside like a second skin. In words measured and
hewn, the poet, in her essential task of making, creates and
articulates and exposes my loneliness for the company that
it is.

The voice in this poem knows that enormous *Dark* allows no room for *Peace*. Heaven forbid that the infidel *Hope*
try to force its bully way in, disrespecting the sacred hall of
Suffering. For three verses, there is no pushing or scolding
or prompting or suggesting a self-help book on grief management. It is pain drawn sacred, deserving of a space measured in cubits, ordained, a sacrament, tended to, shielded
from blasphemy. *Suffering* and *Loneliness* are respected,
exalted.

From the poems that I have kept and read and reread
over the last eight years, I have received or extracted in in-
crements when the whole poem was too weighty or turned
to the next thing too quickly, when what I needed was
strength to stay and be. For years I did not read the last

stanza in this poem. Poems especially lend themselves to fragmentary reading and rereading. I partook of the rare and profound food in the first verses and chose not to taste the delight at the poem's end. At the same time, I could not excise it. I knew it was there.

For several years I kept the fourth stanza folded under. The lining of the pocket in my bag where I tucked the poem turned the crease in the paper red. In the final stanza, the poem turns on its heel and accuses me of enshrouding myself cowardly in the loneliness, the dark fate, the suffering and lying down to die. It indicted me for languishing in misery.

In the last year, the poem for me has become all about the fourth stanza, all about the harder task of reaching for the *Blue Peninsula*, risking delight again in my life given Ike's illness. What might be on *My Blue Peninsula*? What might I be afraid to gain? What might I be conveniently, timidly avoiding by staying encased in painful, familiar, safe victimhood?

Familiar with the wound, I had become a wound. And from there I could render suspect all love, joy, friendship, companionship. I could avoid self-exposure, defer knowing myself or having others venture in. It could be all about my son's illness, how noble. Might happiness or fulfillment or purpose be waiting? Could the desire to reach it bring with it the guts to risk it? As Ike is not his disease, could it be that I am not my sorrow?

I would not have heard the fourth verse had I not

steeped long in the first three. Now that I have read the fourth many times, the *Room Ordained* in the beginning does not read the same. The room is still sacred and set apart, but the door is open. It is not an ultimate destination. Read through, the poem has re-created itself. The *Dark* houses a dare, a goading: *It might be easier / To fail.* From its windows billow challenges to me. Do I have it in me to reach for *Peace, Hope,* even *Delight?* Is there an *Other* to interrupt *my Fate?* Can I answer? Carl Sandburg writes,

> *Let joy kill you.*
> *Keep away from the little deaths.*

Imagine that.

Acknowledgments

Thank you to several people who believed in this writing early on: Marc Patterson, Edward Goldstein, David Lynch, Steve Goyer, the organizers and participants at the Duke Poetry and Medicine Conference in 2004, my writer friends in Abby Thomas's weekly workshop, and my friends and teachers in the Queens M.F.A. program in North Carolina.

Thank you especially to Jonathan Galassi for understanding what I had written better than I did at times and for believing that it might have a life beyond mine with Ike. Thank you to Liz Darhansoff for her support, expertise, and intuition. Thank you to Annie Wedekind for navigating this book to publication with an ever-engaging mix of professional skill and personal respect for the project.

To my friends and family—without you, any shape here visible would not be. My thoughts of you and my thanks for you are inseparable. You have widened my raft. Thank you.

Permissions Acknowledgments

Grateful acknowledgment is made for permission to reprint the following previously published material:

"Poems May Not Geyser," "A Short Account of Longing," and "Grace" from *Origami Bridges: Poems of Psychoanalysis and Fire*, by Diane Ackerman. Copyright © 2002 by Diane Ackerman. Reprinted by permission of HarperCollins Publishers.

"For the Time Being," copyright © 1944 and renewed 1972 by W. H. Auden, from *Collected Poems*, by W. H. Auden. Used by permission of Random House, Inc.

"One Art" from *The Complete Poems 1927–1979*, by Elizabeth Bishop. Copyright © 1979, 1983 by Alice Helen Methfessel. Reprinted by permission of Farrar, Straus and Giroux, LLC.

"Cartography" from *The Blue Estuaries*, by Louise Bogan. Copyright © 1968 by Louise Bogan. Copyright © renewed 1996 by Ruth Limmer. Reprinted by permission of Farrar, Straus and Giroux, LLC.

"How You" and "Speak, You Also" from *Poems of Paul Celan*, translated by Michael Hamburger. Translation copyright © 1972, 1980, 1994, 2002 by Michael Hamburger. Reprinted by permission of Persea Books, Inc. (New York).

"Introduction to Poetry" from *The Apple that Astonished Paris*, by Billy Collins. Copyright © 1998 by Billy Collins. Reprinted with the permission of the University of Arkansas Press, www.uapress.com.

"On Turning Ten" from *The Art of Drowning*, by Billy Collins, copyright © 1995. Reprinted by permission of the University of Pittsburgh Press.

"love is a place," by E. E. Cummings. Copyright © 1935, © 1963, 1991 by the Trustees from the E. E. Cummings Trust. Copyright © 1978 by George James Firmage, from *Complete Poems: 1904–1962*, by E. E. Cummings, edited by George J. Firmage. Used by permission of Liveright Publishing Corporation.

"Bound a trouble," "We learned the whole of love," and "It might be lonelier" reprinted with the permission of the publishers and the Trustees of Amherst College from *The Poems of Emily Dickinson*, Thomas H. Johnson, ed., Cambridge, Mass.: The Belknap Press of Harvard University Press, copyright © 1951, 1955, 1979, 1983 by the President and Fellows of Harvard College.

"A Green Crab's Shell" from *Atlantis*, by Mark Doty. Copyright © 1995 by Mark Doty. Reprinted by permission of HarperCollins Publishers.

"Bereft" and "Devotion" from *The Poetry of Robert Frost*, edited by Edward Connery Lathem. Copyright © 1928, 1969 by Henry Holt and Company, copyright © 1956 by Robert Frost. Reprinted by permission of Henry Holt and Company, LLC.

"Formaggio" from *Vita Nova*, by Louise Glück. Copyright © 1999 by Louise Glück. Reprinted by permission of HarperCollins Publishers.

Excerpt from "Ardor" from the *The Painted Bed: Poems by Donald Hall*. Copyright © 2002 by Donald Hall. Reprinted by permission of Houghton Mifflin Company. All rights reserved.

"Mr. Cogito" from *Elegy for the Departure*, by Zbigniew Herbert and translated by John and Bogdana Carpenter. Copyright © 1999 by John and Bogdana Carpenter. Reprinted by permission of HarperCollins Publishers.

"What the Living Do,"from *What the Living Do*, by Marie Howe. Copyright © 1997 by Marie Howe. Used by permission of W. W. Norton & Company, Inc.

"Disenfranchised, Grieving" copyright © by Lynn Kilpatrick. First published in *Tin House Magazine* #17, Fall 2003.

"To 'Yes' " from *Collected Poems of Kenneth Koch*, copyright © 2005 by the Kenneth Koch Literary Estate. Used by permission of Alfred A. Knopf, a division of Random House, Inc.

Excerpt from "The End" from *Amores*, by D. H. Lawrence. Copyright © 1916 by the estate of Frieda Lawrence Ravagli. Reproduced with permission of the proprietor and Pollinger Limited.

"Last Night, As I Was Sleeping," by Antonio Machado, translated by Robert Bly, copyright © by Robert Bly. From *Times Alone: Selected Poems of Antonio Machado* (Wesleyan University Press, 1983).

"The Human Heart" from *Pax Atomica*, by Campbell McGrath. Copyright © 2004 by Campbell McGrath. Reprinted by permission of HarperCollins Publishers.

Excerpts from "Renascence" by Edna St. Vincent Millay. Copyright © 1912, 1940 by Edna St. Vincent Millay. Reprinted by permission of Elizabeth Barnett, literary executor, the Millay Society.

"Early Darkness" copyright © 2001 by D. Patrick Miller. Reprinted from *Instructions of the Spirit: Poems and Intimations*, Fearless Books, 2004 (www.fearlessbooks.com).

"On Prayer" from *The Collected Poems* 1931–1987, by Czeslaw Milosz. Copyright © 1988 by Czeslaw Milosz Royalties, Inc. Reprinted by permission of HarperCollins Publishers.

"What Are Years" reprinted with the permission of Scribner, an imprint of Simon and Schuster Adult Publishing Group, from *Collected Poems*, by Marianne Moore. Copyright © 1941 by Marianne Moore; copyright renewed © 1969 by Marianne Moore. Open market rights granted with permission of Faber and Faber Ltd, from *The Poems of Marianne Moore*, edited by Grace Schulman.

"My Heart" from *Collected Poems*, by Frank O'Hara, copyright © 1971 by Maureen Granville-Smith, administratrix of the Estate of Frank O'Hara. Used by permission of Alfred A. Knopf, a division of Random House, Inc.

"His Stillness" from *The Father*, by Sharon Olds, copyright © 1992 by Sharon Olds. Used by permission of Alfred A. Knopf, a division of Random House, Inc.

"Text" from *Love Song with Motor Vehicles*, by Alan Michael Parker. Copyright © 2003 by Alan Michael Parker. Reprinted with the permission of BOA Editions, Ltd., www.BOAEditions.org.

"A Gesture" from *Cornucopia: New and Selected Poems*, by Molly Peacock. Copyright © 2002 by Molly Peacock. Used by permission of W. W. Norton & Company, Inc.

"A Mathematics of Breathing" copyright © 1995 by Carl Phillips. Reprinted from *Cortege* with the permission of Graywolf Press, Saint Paul, Minnesota.

"Delta," copyright © 1989, 2002 by Adrienne Rich, from *The Fact of a Doorframe: Selected Poems 1950–2001*, by Adrienne Rich. Used by permission of the author and W. W. Norton & Company, Inc.

"Sunset" from *Selected Poems of Rainer Maria Rilke, A Translation from the German and Commentary*, by Robert Bly. Copyright © 1981 by Robert Bly. Reprinted by permission of HarperCollins Publishers.

"The Well of Grief" from *Where the Many Rivers Meet* by David Whyte. Copyright © 1990, 2004 by David Whyte. Used by permission of the author and Many Rivers Press (www.davidwhyte.com). Excerpt from "The House of Belonging" from the *The House of Belonging*, by David

Whyte. Copyright © 1997, 2004 by David Whyte. Used by permission of the author and Many Rivers Press (www.davidwhyte.com). Excerpt from "The Poet" from *Fire in the Earth*, by David Whyte. Copyright © 1992, 2002 by David Whyte. Used by permission of the author and Many Rivers Press (www.davidwhyte.com).

"Tantrum" from *Repair*, by C. K. Williams. Copyright © 1999 by C. K. Williams. Reprinted by permission of Farrar, Straus and Giroux, LLC.

"The Stare's Nest by My Window" reprinted with the permission of Scribner, an imprint of Simon & Schuster Adult Publishing Group, from *The Collected Works of W. B. Yeats, Volume I: The Poems, Revised*, edited by Richard J. Finneran. Copyright © 1928 by The Macmillan Company; copyright renewed © 1956 by Georgie Yeats. Open Market given by permission of A. P. Watt Ltd. on behalf of Michael B. Yeats.

WALTHAM
PUBLIC LIBRARY